The John Dewey Essays
in Philosophy

Edited by the Department
of Philosophy,
Columbia University,
and including
the John Dewey Lectures

Number One

Ontological
Relativity and
Other Essays

Ontological Relativity and Other Essays

by W. V. Quine

Columbia University Press

New York and London

1969

This volume consists of the first of the John Dewey Lectures delivered at Columbia University under the auspices of the Department of Philosophy and five additional essays. W. V. Quine is Edgar Pierce Professor of Philosophy at Harvard University

Copyright © 1969 W. V. Quine
SBN-231-03307-9
Library of Congress Catalog Card Number: 72-91121
Printed in the United States of America

Preface

The title essay of this book was presented as a pair of lectures of the same title at Columbia University, March 26 and 28, 1968. They constituted the first of the John Dewey Lectures, which are to be delivered biennially. Dewey was professor of philosophy at Columbia from 1905 until 1930.

A week after I gave the second lecture, the two lectures appeared by permission of Columbia University as an article in the *Journal of Philosophy*. I have since corrected and expanded one remark; the improvement comes in pages 56*f* and 61, where seven lines of old text have given way to a page and a half of new. Michael Jubien found the error.

I had given a single lecture under the same title at Yale and the University of Chicago as early as May 1967, but it was no near approach to what is now before us. My thoughts on the matter matured appreciably in the intervening ten months.

To help orient the reader, the title essay is preceded in the volume by "Speaking of Objects." This was my presidential address to the eastern division of the American Philosophical Association in 1957, and it is reprinted from the association's *Proceedings and Addresses,* 1958, with permission. This essay stemmed from my work in progress, which in 1960 became *Word and Object.* Considerable parts of Sections II and III of "Speaking of Objects" recur verbatim in Sections 19 and 25 of *Word and Object,* and other parts of the essay recur in that book in substance. For that reason I omitted "Speaking of Objects" from my recent collection *The Ways of Paradox and Other Essays,* and had meant to omit it from the present volume.

However, Burton Dreben has persuaded me that "Speaking of Objects" is strangely efficacious in giving readers a better understanding of what I was up to in *Word and Object.* He finds moreover that students and other critics of *Word and Object* are largely unaware of "Speaking of Objects," despite its having been anthologized three times in English and once in Spanish. Appreciating as I do how well Dreben understands my point of view and how effective he has been at interpreting it, I am following his advice and reprinting the essay intact.

The remaining four essays in the book are of recent vintage. They were already at press before this book was thought of, and they still are. Some of them will doubtless appear, in their several original places, ahead of this book.

The first of the four—hence the third of the six—is "Epistemology Naturalized." I presented it at Vienna on September 9, 1968, as an invited address to the Fourteenth International Congress of Philosophy. It is to appear in the acts of that congress, and is included in the present book by permission of the secretary of the congress. At the middle of the essay a few lines have been dropped in favor of cross-references to other parts of the book. A similar deletion has been made at the end and at an intermediate point, and a note inserted.

Large portions of "Epistemology Naturalized" were adapted from an unpublished Arnold Isenberg Memorial Lecture that I gave at Michigan State University on November 19, 1965, under the title "Stimulus and Meaning." Therefore "Epistemology Naturalized" should be seen as dedicated to the memory of Arnold Isenberg, as is "Ontological Relativity" to the memory of John Dewey.

The fourth essay, "Existence and Quantification," was prepared for a colloquium held at the University of Western Ontario, November 4, 1966. On that day the plane which was taking me to meet my audience was forced down by a storm. But Joseph Margolis had prudently obtained an advance copy of my paper, and this he read to my audience while I languished in Buffalo. I subsequently read the paper at Princeton and Brandeis, and it has improved. The present version is about to appear in the colloquium volume, *Fact and Existence*. It is reprinted here by kind permission of Basil Blackwell and the University of Toronto Press, who hold the copyright, and Joseph Margolis. It is also about to appear, by similar permission, in the new quarterly *l'Age de la Science*.

The fifth, "Natural Kinds," is dedicated to Carl G. Hempel. I trust that by the time this book comes out there will no longer be a breach of security in saying that Alan Ross Anderson has been editing a *Festschrift* for Hempel. I wrote "Natural Kinds" for that volume, and that is where the copyright goes. Meanwhile I am including it here with Anderson's kind permission. I read earlier drafts of this paper as lectures at Long Island University, Brooklyn, October 17, 1967, and the University of Connecticut, December 7.

The sixth and last, "Propositional Objects," is a lecture that

I gave at Amherst College, the University of Michigan, the University of Chicago, and the University of Illinois at Urbana in the spring of 1965. It is about to appear in *Critica*, and is reprinted here with the permission of the editors of that quarterly.

W. V. Q.

Cambridge, Mass.
November, 1968

Contents

1

Speaking of Objects

I

We are prone to talk and think of objects. Physical objects are the obvious illustration when the illustrative mood is on us, but there are also all the abstract objects, or so there purport to be: the states and qualities, numbers, attributes, classes. We persist in breaking reality down somehow into a multiplicity of identifiable and discriminable objects, to be referred to by singular and general terms. We talk so inveterately of objects that to say we do so seems almost to say nothing at all; for how else is there to talk?

It is hard to say how else there is to talk, not because our objectifying pattern is an invariable trait of human nature, but because we are bound to adapt any alien pattern to our own in the very process of understanding or translating the alien sentences.

Imagine a newly discovered tribe whose language is without known affinities. The linguist has to learn the language directly by observing what the natives say under observed circumstances, encountered or contrived. He makes a first crude beginning by compiling native terms for environing objects; but here already he is really imposing his own patterns. Let me explain what I mean. I will grant that the linguist may establish inductively, beyond reasonable doubt, that a certain heathen expression is one to which natives can be prompted to assent by the presence of a rabbit, or reasonable *facsimile,* and not otherwise. The linguist is then warranted in according the native expression the cautious translation "There's a rabbit," "There we have a rabbit," "Lo! a rabbit," "Lo! rabbithood again," insofar as the differences among these English sentences are counted irrelevant. This much translation can be objective, however exotic the tribe. It recognizes the native expression as in effect a rabbit-heralding sentence. But the linguist's bold further step, in which he imposes his own object-positing pattern without special warrant, is taken when he equates the native expression or any part of it with the *term* "rabbit."

It is easy to show that such appeal to an object category is unwarranted even though we cannot easily, in English, herald rabbits without objectification. For we can argue from indifference. Given that a native sentence says that a so-and-so is present, and given that the sentence is true when and only when a rabbit is present, it by no means follows that the so-and-so are rabbits. They might be all the various temporal segments of rabbits. They might be all the integral or undetached parts of rabbits. In order to decide among these alternatives we need to be able to ask more than whether a so-and-so is present. We need to be able to ask whether this is the same so-and-so as that, and whether one so-and-so is present or two. We need something like the apparatus of identity and quantification; hence far more than we are in a position to avail ourselves of in a language in which our high point as of even date is rabbit-announcing.

And the case is yet worse: we do not even have evidence for taking the native expression as of the form "A so-and-so is present"; it could as well be construed with an abstract singular term, as meaning that rabbithood is locally manifested. Better just "Rabbiteth," like "Raineth."

But if our linguist is going to be as cagey as all this, he will never translate more than these simple-minded announcements of observable current events. A cagey linguist is a caged linguist. What we want from the linguist as a serviceable finished product, after all, is no mere list of sentence-to-sentence equivalences, like the airline throwaways of useful Spanish phrases. We want a manual of instructions for custom-building a native sentence to roughly the purpose of any newly composed English sentence, within reason, and vice versa. The linguist has to resolve the potential infinity of native sentences into a manageably limited list of grammatical constructions and constituent linguistic forms, and then show how the business of each can be approximated in English; and vice versa. Sometimes perhaps he will translate a word or construction not directly but contextually, by systematic instructions for translating its containing sentences; but still he must make do with a limited lot of contextual definitions. Now once he has carried out this necessary job of lexicography, forwards and backwards, he has read our ontological point of view into the native language. He has decided what expressions to treat as referring to objects, and, within limits, what sorts of objects to treat them as referring to. He has had to decide, however arbitrarily, how to accommodate English idioms of identity and quantification in native translation.

The word "arbitrary" needs stressing, not because those decisions are wholly arbitrary, but because they are so much more so than one tends to suppose. For, what evidence does

the linguist have? He started with what we may call native observation sentences, such as the rabbit announcement. These
he can say how to translate into English, provided we impute
no relevance to the differences between "Here a rabbit," "Here
rabbithood," and the like. Also he can record further native
sentences and settle whether various persons are prepared to
affirm or deny them, though he find no rabbit movements or
other currently observable events to tie them to. Among these
untranslated sentences he may get an occasional hint of logical
connections, by finding say that just the persons who are prepared to affirm A are prepared to affirm B and deny C. There-
after his data leave off and his creativity sets in.

What he does in his creativity is attribute special and distinctive functions to component words, or conspicuously recurrent fragments, of the recorded sentences. The only ways one
can appraise these attributions are as follows. One can see
whether they add up to representing the rabbit sentence and
the like as conforming to their previously detected truth conditions. One can see also how well they fit the available data on
other sentences: sentences for which no truth conditions are
known, but only the varying readiness of natives to affirm or
deny them. Beyond this we can judge the attributions only on
their simplicity and naturalness—to *us*.

Certainly the linguist will try out his theory on the natives,
springing new sentences authorized by his theory, to see if
they turn out right. This is a permuting of the time order: one
frames the theory before all possible data are in, and then lets
it guide one in the eliciting of additional data likeliest to matter. This is good scientific method, but it opens up no new kind
of data. English general and singular terms, identity, quantification, and the whole bag of ontological tricks may be corre-
lated with elements of the native language in any of various

mutually incompatible ways, each compatible with all possible linguistic data, and none preferable to another save as favored by a rationalization of the *native* language that is simple and natural to *us*.

It makes no real difference that the linguist will turn bilingual and come to think as the natives do—whatever that means. For the arbitrariness of reading our objectifications into the heathen speech reflects not so much the inscrutability of the heathen mind, as that there is nothing to scrute. Even we who grew up together and learned English at the same knee, or adjacent ones, talk alike for no other reason than that society coached us alike in a pattern of verbal response to externally observable cues. We have been beaten into an outward conformity to an outward standard; and thus it is that when I correlate your sentences with mine by the simple rule of phonetic correspondence, I find that the public circumstances of your affirmations and denials agree pretty well with those of my own. If I conclude that you share my sort of conceptual scheme, I am not adding a supplementary conjecture so much as spurning unfathomable distinctions; for, what further criterion of sameness of conceptual scheme can be imagined? The case of a Frenchman, moreover, is the same except that I correlate his sentences with mine not by phonetic correspondence but according to a traditionally evolved dictionary.[1] The case of the linguist and his newly discovered heathen, finally, differs simply in that the linguist has to grope for a general sentence-to-sentence correlation that will make the public circumstances of the heathen's affirmations and denials match up tolerably with the circumstances of the linguist's own. If the linguist fails in this, or has a hard time of it, or succeeds only by dint of an

[1] See Richard von Mises, *Positivism*, Cambridge: Harvard, 1951, pp. 46 ff.

ugly and complex mass of correlations, then he is entitled to say—in the only sense in which one *can* say it—that his heathens have a very different attitude toward reality from ours; and even so he cannot coherently suggest what their attitude is. Nor, in principle, is the natural bilingual any better off.

When we compare theories, doctrines, points of view, and cultures, on the score of what sorts of objects there are said to be, we are comparing them in a respect which itself makes sense only provincially. It makes sense only as far afield as our efforts to translate our domestic idioms of identity and quantification bring encouragement in the way of simple and natural-looking correspondences. If we attend to business we are unlikely to find a very alien culture with a predilection for a very outlandish universe of discourse, just because the outlandishness of it would detract from our sense of patness of our dictionary of translation. There is a notion that our provincial ways of positing objects and conceiving nature may be best appreciated for what they are by standing off and seeing them against a cosmopolitan background of alien cultures; but the notion comes to nothing, for there is no ποῦ στῶ.[2]

II

Yet, for all the difficulty of transcending our object-directed pattern of thought, we can examine it well enough from inside. Let us turn our attention from the heathen, who seemed to have a term for "rabbit," to our own child at home who seems

[2] For a fuller development of the foregoing theme see my "Meaning and translation" in Reuben Brower's anthology *On Translation* (Harvard, at press). For criticisms that have benefitted the above section of the present essay and ensuing portions I am grateful to Burton Dreben.

to have just acquired his first few terms in our own language: "mama," "water," perhaps "red." To begin with, the case of the child resembles that of the heathen. For though we may fully satisfy ourselves that the child has learned the trick of using the utterances "mama" and "water" strictly in the appropriate presences, or as means of inducing the appropriate presences, still we have no right to construe these utterances in the child's mouth as terms, at first, for things or substances.

We in our maturity have come to look upon the child's mother as an integral body who, in an irregular closed orbit, revisits the child from time to time; and to look upon red in a radically different way, viz., as scattered about. Water, for us, is rather like red, but not quite; things can be red, but only stuff is water. But the mother, red, and water are for the infant all of a type: each is just a history of sporadic encounter, a scattered portion of what goes on. His first learning of the three words is uniformly a matter of learning how much of what goes on about him counts as the mother, or as red, or as water. It is not for the child to say in the first case "Hello! mama again," in the second case "Hello! another red thing," and in the third case "Hello! more water." They are all on a par: Hello! more mama, more red, more water. Even this last formula, which treats all three terms on the model of our provincial adult bulk term "water," is imperfect; for it unwarrantedly imputes an objectification of matter, even if only as stuff and not as bits.

Progressively, however, the child is seen to evolve a pattern of verbal behavior that finally comes to copy ours too closely for there to be any sense in questioning the general sameness of conceptual scheme. For perspective on our own objectifying apparatus we may consider what steps of development make the difference between the "mama"-babbling infant who cannot be said to be using terms for objects, and the older child who can.

It is only when the child has got on to the full and proper use of *individuative* terms like "apple" that he can properly be said to have taken to using terms as terms, and speaking of objects. Words like "apple," and not words like "mama" or "water" or "red," are the terms whose ontological involvement runs deep. To learn "apple" it is not sufficient to learn how much of what goes on counts as apple; we must learn how much counts as *an* apple, and how much as another. Such terms possess built-in modes of individuation.

Individuative terms are commonly made to double as bulk terms. Thus we may say "There is some apple in the salad," not meaning "some apple or other"; just as we may say "Mary had a little lamb" in either of two senses. Now we have appreciated that the child can learn the terms "mama," "red," and "water" quite well before he ever has mastered the ins and outs of our adult conceptual scheme of mobile enduring physical objects, identical from time to time and place to place; and in principle he might do the same for "apple," as a bulk term for uncut apple stuff. But he can never fully master "apple" in its individuative use, except as he gets on with the scheme of enduring and recurrent physical objects. He may come somewhat to grips with the individuative use of "apple" before quite mastering the comprehensive physical outlook, but his usage will be marred by misidentifications of distinct apples over time, or misdiscriminations of identical ones.

He has really got on to the individuative use, one is tempted to suppose, once he responds with the plural "apples" to a heap of apples. But not so. He may at that point have learned "apples" as another bulk term, applicable to just so much apple as is taken up in apple heaps. "Apples," for him, would be subordinated to "apple" as is "warm water" to "water," and "bright red" to "red."

The child might proceed to acquire "block" and "blocks," "ball" and "balls," as bulk terms in the same fashion. By the force of analogy among such pairs he might even come to apply the plural "-s" with seeming appropriateness to new words, and to drop it with seeming appropriateness from words first learned only with it. We might well not detect, for a while, his misconception: that "-s" just turns bulk terms into more specialized bulk terms connoting clumpiness.

A plausible variant misconception is this: "apple" bulkwise might cover just the apple stuff that is spaced off in lone apples, while "apples" still figures as last suggested. Then apples and apple would be mutually exclusive rather than subordinate the one to the other. This variant misconception could likewise be projected systematically to "block" and "blocks," "ball" and "balls," and long escape exposure.

How can we ever tell, then, whether the child has really got the trick of individuation? Only by engaging him in sophisticated discourse of "that apple," "not that apple," "an apple," "same apple," "another apple," "these apples." It is only at this level that a palpable difference emerges between genuinely individuative use and the conterfeits lately imagined.

Doubtless the child gets the swing of these peculiar adjectives "same," "another," "an," "that," "not that," contextually: first he become attuned to various longer phrases or sentences that contain them, and then gradually he develops appropriate habits in relation to the component words as common parts and residues of those longer forms. His tentative acquisition of the plural "-s," lately speculated on, is itself a first primitive step of the kind. The contextual learning of these various particles goes on simultaneously, we may suppose, so that they are gradually adjusted to one another and a coherent pattern of usage is evolved matching that of one's elders. This is a major step in acquiring the conceptual scheme that we all know so well. For it is on achieving this step, and only then, that there can be any general talk of objects as such. Only at this stage does it begin to make sense to wonder whether the apple now in one's hand is the apple noticed yesterday.

Until individuation emerges, the child can scarcely be said to have general *or* singular terms, there being no express talk of objects. The pre-individuative term "mama," and likewise "water" and "red" (for children who happen to learn "water" and "red" before mastering individuation), hark back to a primitive phase to which the distinction between singular and general is irrelevant. Once the child has pulled through the individuative crisis, though, he is prepared to reassess prior terms. "Mama," in particular, gets set up retroactively as the name of a broad and recurrent but withal individual object, and thus as a singular term *par excellence*. Occasions eliciting "mama" being just as discontinuous as those eliciting "water," the two terms had been on a par; but with the advent of individuation the mother becomes integrated into a cohesive spatiotemporal convexity, while water remains scattered even in space-time. The two terms thus part company.

The mastery of individuation seems scarcely to affect people's attitude toward "water." For "water," "sugar," and the like the category of bulk terms remains, a survival of the pre-individuative phase, ill fitting the dichotomy into general and singular. But the philosophical mind sees its way to pressing this archaic category into the dichotomy. The bulk term "water" after the copula can usually be smoothly reconstrued as a general term true of each portion of water, while in other positions it is usually more simply construed as a singular term naming that spatiotemporally diffuse object which is the totality of the world's water.

III

I have urged that we could know the necessary and sufficient stimulatory conditions of every possible act of utterance, in a foreign language, and still not know how to determine what objects the speakers of that language believe in. Now if objective reference is so inaccessible to observation, who is to say on empirical grounds that belief in objects of one or another description is right or wrong? How can there ever be empirical evidence against existential statements?

The answer is something like this. Grant that a knowledge of the appropriate stimulatory conditions of a sentence does not settle how to construe the sentence in terms of existence of objects. Still, it does tend to settle what is to count as empirical evidence for or against the truth of the sentence. If we then go on to assign the sentence some import in point of existence of objects, by arbitrary projection in the case of the heathen language or as a matter of course in the case of our own, thereupon what has already been counting as empirical evidence for or against the truth of the sentence comes to count as empirical evidence for or against the existence of the objects.

The opportunity for error in existential statements increases with one's mastery of the verbal apparatus of objective reference. In one's earliest phase of word learning, terms like "mama" and "water" were learned which may be viewed retrospectively as names each of an observed spatiotemporal object. Each such term was learned by a process of reinforcement and extinction, whereby the spatiotemporal range of application of the term was gradually perfected. The object named is assuredly an observed one, in the sense that the reinforced stimuli proceeded pretty directly from it. Granted, this talk of name and object belongs to a later phase of language learning, even as does the talk of stimulation.

The second phase, marked by the advent of individuative terms, is where a proper notion of object emerges. Here we get general terms, each true of each of many objects. But the objects still are observable spatiotemporal objects. For these individuative terms, e.g. "apple," are learned still by the old method of reinforcement and extinction; they differ from their predecessors only in the added feature of internal individuation.

Demonstrative singular terms like "this apple" usher in a third phase, characterized by the fact that a singular term seriously used can now, through error, fail to name: the thing pointed to can turn out to be the mere façade of an apple, or maybe a tomato. But even at this stage anything that we do succeed in naming is still an observable spatiotemporal object.

A fourth phase comes with the joining of one general term to another in attributive position. Now for the first time we can get general terms which are not true of anything; thus "blue apple," "square ball." But when there are things at all of which the thus formed general terms are true, they are still nothing new; they are just some among the same old observables whereof the component terms are true.

It is a fifth phase that brings a new mode of understanding, giving access to new sorts of objects. When we form compounds by applying relative terms to singular terms, we get such compounds as "smaller than that speck." Whereas the non-existence of observable blue apples is tantamount to the non-existence of blue apples, the non-existence of observable objects smaller than that speck is not taken as tantamount to the non-existence of objects smaller than that speck. The notable feature of this fifth phase is not that it enables us to form meaningful singular terms devoid of reference, for that was already achieved on occasion with "this apple"; nor that it enables us to form meaningful general terms true of nothing, for that was already achieved with "blue apple"; but that it enables us, for the first time, to form terms whose references can be admitted to be forever unobservable without yet being repudiated, like blue apples, as non-existent.

Such applying of relative terms to singular terms is the simplest method of forming terms that purport to name unobservables, but there are also more flexible devices to much the same effect: the relative clause and description.

And there comes yet a sixth phase, when we break through to posits more drastically new still than the objects smaller than the smallest visible speck. For the objects smaller than the speck differ from observable objects only in a matter of degree, whereas the sixth phase ushers in abstract entities. This phase is marked by the advent of abstract singular terms like "redness," "roundness," "mankind," purported names of qualities, attributes, classes. Let us speculate on the mechanism of this new move.

One wedge is the bulk term. Such terms can be learned at the very first phase, we saw, on a par with "mama." We saw them diverge from "mama" at the second phase, simply on the score that the woman comes then to be appreciated as an integrated spatiotemporal thing while the world's water or red stuff ordinarily does not. For the child, thus, who is not on to the sophisticated idea of the scattered single object, the bulk term already has an air of generality about it, comparable to the individuative "apple"; and still it is much like the singular "mama" in form and function, having even been learned or learnable at the first phase on a par with "mama." So the bulk term already has rather the hybrid air of the abstract singular term. "Water" might, from the very advent of individuation, even be said to name a shared *attribute* of the sundry puddles and glassfuls rather than a scattered portion of the world *composed* of those puddles and glassfuls; for the child of course adopts neither position.

Moreover, there is a tricky point about color words that especially encourages the transition to abstract reference. "Red" can be learned as a bulk term, like "water," but in particular it applies to apples whose insides are white. Before mastering the conceptual scheme of individuation and enduring physical object, the child sees the uncut red apple, like tomato juice, simply as so much red exposure in the passing show, and, having no sense of physical identity, he sees the subsequently exposed white interior of the apple as irrelevant. When eventually he does master the conceptual scheme of individuation and enduring physical object, then, he has to come to terms with a preacquired use of "red" that has suddenly gone double: there is red stuff (tomato juice) and there are red things (apples) that are mostly white stuff. "Red" both remains a bulk term of the ancient vintage of "water" and "mama," and becomes a concrete general term like "round" or "apple." Since the child will still not clearly conceive of "red" as suddenly two words, we have him somehow infusing singularity into the concrete general; and such is the recipe, however unappetizing, for the abstract singular. The analogy then spreads to other general terms, that were in no such special predicament as "red," until they all deliver abstract singulars.

Another force for abstract terms, or for the positing of abstract objects, lies in abbreviated cross-reference. E.g., after an elaborate remark regarding President Eisenhower, someone says: "The same holds for Churchill." Or, by way of supporting some botanical identification, one says: "Both plants have the following attribute in common"—and proceeds with a double-purpose description. In such cases a laborious repetition is conveniently circumvented. Now the cross-reference in such cases is just to a form of words. But we have a stubborn tendency to reify the unrepeated matter by positing an attribute, instead of just talking of words.

There is indeed an archaic precedent for confusing sign and object; the earliest conditioning of the infant's babbling is ambiguous on the point. For suppose a baby rewarded for happening to babble something like "mama" or "water" just as the mother or water is looming. The stimuli which are thus re-inforced are bound to be two: there is not only the looming of the object, there is equally the word itself, heard by the child from his own lips. Confusion of sign and object is original sin, coeval with the word.

We have seen how the child might slip into the community's ontology of attributes by easy stages, from bulk terms onward. We have also seen how talk of attributes will continue to be encouraged, in the child and the community, by a certain convenience of cross-reference coupled with a confusion of sign and object. We have in these reflections some materials for speculation regarding the early beginnings of an ontology of attributes in the childhood of the race. There is room, as well, for alternative or supplementary conjectures; e.g., that the attributes are vestiges of the minor deities of some creed outworn.[3] In a general way such speculation is epistemologically relevant, as suggesting how organisms maturing and evolving

[3] Thus Ernst Cassirer, *Language and Myth* (New York: Harper, 1946), pp. 95 ff.

in the physical environment we know might conceivably end up discoursing of abstract objects as we do. But the disreputability of origins is of itself no argument against preserving and prizing the abstract ontology. This conceptual scheme may well be, however accidental, a happy accident; just as the theory of electrons would be none the worse for having first occurred to its originator in the course of some absurd dream. At any rate the ontology of abstract objects is part of the ship which, in Neurath's figure, we are rebuilding at sea.[4] We may revise the scheme, but only in favor of some clearer or simpler and no less adequate overall account of what goes on in the world.

IV

By finding out roughly which non-verbal stimulations tend to prompt assent to a given existential statement, we settle, to some degree, what is to count as empirical evidence for or against the existence of the objects in question. This I urged at the beginning of III. Statements, however, existential and otherwise, vary in the directness with which they are conditioned to non-verbal stimulation. Commonly a stimulation will trigger our verdict on a statement only because the statement is a strand in the verbal network of some elaborate theory, other strands of which are more directly conditioned to that stimulation. Most of our statements respond thus to reverberations across the fabric of intralinguistic associations, even when also directly conditioned to extralinguistic stimuli to some degree. Highly theoretical statements are statements whose connection with extralinguistic stimulation consists pretty exclusively in the reverberations across the fabric. Statements of the

---

[4] Otto Neurath, "Protokollsätze," *Erkenntnis* 3 (1932), 206.

existence of various sorts of subvisible particles tend to be theoretical, in this sense; and, even more so, statements of the existence of certain abstract objects. Commonly such statements are scarcely to be judged otherwise than by coherence, or by considerations of overall simplicity of a theory whose ultimate contacts with experience are remote as can be from the statements in question. Yet, remarkably enough, there are abstract existence statements that do succumb to such considerations. We have had the wit to posit an ontology massive enough to crumble of its own weight.

For there are the paradoxes of classes. These paradoxes are usually stated for classes because classes are a relatively simple kind of abstract object to talk about, and also because classes, being more innocent on the face of them than attributes, are more fun to discredit. In any event, as is both well known and obvious, the paradoxes of classes go through *pari passu* for attributes, and again for relations.

The moral to draw from the paradoxes is not necessarily nominalism, but certainly that we must tighten our ontological belts a few holes. The law of attributes that was implicit in our language habits or that fitted in with them most easily was that *every* statement that mentions a thing attributes an attribute to it; and this cultural heritage, however venerable, must go. Some judicious *ad hoc* excisions are required at least.

Systematic considerations can press not only for repudiating certain objects, and so declaring certain *terms* irreferential; they can also press for declaring certain *occurrences* of terms irreferential, while other occurrences continue to refer. This point is essentially Frege's,[5] and an example is provided by the

---

[5] See Frege, "On sense and reference," translated in *Philosophical Writings of Gottlob Frege* (Geach and Black, eds.), Oxford: Blackwell, 1952, and in *Readings in Philosophical Analysis* (Feigl and Sellars, eds.), New York: Appleton, 1949. See also my *From a Logical Point of View,* Cambridge: Harvard, 1953, Essay 8.

sentence "Tom believes that Tully wrote the *Ars Magna.*" If we assert this on the strength of Tom's confusion of Tully with Lully, and in full appreciation of Tom's appreciation that Cicero did not write the *Ars Magna,* then we are not giving the term "Tully" purely referential occurrence in our sentence "Tom believes that Tully wrote the *Ars Magna*"; our sentence is not squarely about Tully. If it were, it would have to be true of Cicero, who *is* Tully.

It was only after somehow deciding what heathen locutions to construe as identity and the like that our linguist could begin to say which heathen words serve as terms and what objects they refer to. It was only after getting the knack of identity and kindred devices that our own child could reasonably be said to be talking in terms and to be talking of objects. And it is to the demands of identity still, specifically the substitutivity of identity, that the adult speaker of our language remains answerable as long as he may be said to be using terms to refer.

We are free so to use the verb "believes" as to allow ensuing terms full referential status after all. To do so is to deny "Tom believes that Tully wrote the *Ars Magna*" in the light of Tom's knowledge of Cicero and despite his confusion of names. The fact is that we can and do use "believes" both ways: one way when we say that Tom believes that Tully wrote the *Ars Magna,* and the other way when we deny this, or when, resorting to quantification, we say just that there is *someone* whom Tom believes to have done thus and so. Parallel remarks are suited also to others of the *propositional attitudes,* as Russell calls them: thus doubting, wishing, and striving, along with believing.

Man in a state of nature is not aware of the doubleness of these usages of his, nor of the strings attached to each; just as he is not aware of the paradoxical consequences of a naïve ontology of classes or attributes. Now yet another ontological weakness that we are likewise unaware of until, philosophically minded, we start looking to coherence considerations, has to do with the individuation of attributes.

The positing of attributes is accompanied by no clue as to the circumstances under which attributes may be said to be the same or different. This is perverse, considering that the very use of terms and the very positing of objects are unrecognizable to begin with except as keyed in with idioms of sameness and difference. What happens is that at first we learn general patterns of term-talk and thing-talk with the help of the necessary adjuncts of identity; afterward we project these well-learned grammatical forms to attributes, without settling identity for them. We understand the forms as referential just because they are grammatically analogous to ones that we learned earlier, for physical objects, with full dependence on the identity aspect.

The lack of a proper identity concept for attributes is a lack that philosophers feel impelled to supply; for, what sense is there in saying that there are attributes when there is no sense in saying when there is one attribute and when two? Carnap and others have proposed this principle for identifying attributes: two sentences about x attribute the *same* attribute to x if and only if the two sentences are not merely alike in truth value for each choice of x, but necessarily and analytically so, by sameness of meaning.[6]

However, this formulation depends on a questionable notion, that of sameness of meaning. For let us not slip back into the fantasy of a gallery of ideas and labels. Let us remember rather our field lexicographer's predicament: how arbitrary his

[6] Rudolf Carnap, *Meaning and Necessity*, Chicago, 1947, p. 23.

projection of analogies from known languages. Can an empiricist speak seriously of sameness of meaning of two conditions upon an object x, one stated in the heathen language and one in ours, when even the singling out of an object x as object at all for the heathen language is so hopelessly arbitrary?

We could skip the heathen language and try talking of sameness of meaning just within our own language. This would degrade the ontology of attributes; identity of attributes would be predicated on frankly provincial traits of English usage, ill fitting the objectivity of true objects. Nor let it be said in extenuation that all talk of objects, physical ones included, is in a way provincial too; for the way is different. Our physics is provincial only in that there is no universal basis for translating it into remote languages; it would still never condone defining physical identity in terms of verbal behavior. If we rest the identity of attributes on an admittedly local relation of English synonymy, then we count attributes secondary to language in a way that physical objects are not.

Shall we just let attributes be thus secondary to language in a way that physical objects are not? But our troubles do not end here; for the fact is that I see no hope of making reasonable sense of sameness of meaning even for English. The difficulty is one that I have enlarged on elsewhere.[7] English expressions are supposed to mean the same if, vaguely speaking, you can use one for the other in any situation and any English context without *relevant* difference of effect; and the essential difficulty comes in delimiting the required sense of relevant.

[7] "Two dogmas of empiricism," *Philosophical Review* 60 (1951), 20-43; reprinted in my *From a Logical Point of View.* See further my "Carnap e la verità logica," *Rivista di Filosofia* 48 (1957), 3-29, which is a translation of an essay whereof part has appeared also in the original English under the title "Logical truth" in *American Philosophers at Work* (Sidney Hook, ed.), New York: Criterion, 1956.

V

There is no denying the access of power that accrues to our conceptual scheme through the positing of abstract objects. Most of what is gained by positing attributes, however, is gained equally by positing classes. Classes are on a par with attributes on the score of abstractness or universality, and they serve the purposes of attributes so far as mathematics and certainly most of science are concerned; and they enjoy, unlike attributes, a crystal-clear identity concept. No wonder that in mathematics the murky intensionality of attributes tends to give way to the limpid extensionality of classes; and likewise in other sciences, roughly in proportion to the rigor and austerity of their systematization.

For attributes one might still claim this advantage over classes: they help in systematizing what we may call the *attributary attitudes*—hunting, wanting, fearing, lacking, and the like. For, take hunting. Lion hunting is not, like lion catching, a transaction between men and individual lions; for it requires no lions. We analyze lion catching, rabbit catching, etc. as having a catching relation in common and varying only in the individuals caught; but what of lion hunting, rabbit hunting, etc.? If any common relation is to be recognized here, the varying objects of the relation must evidently be taken not as individuals but as kinds. Yet not kinds in the sense of classes, for then unicorn hunting would cease to differ from griffin hunting. Kinds rather in the sense of attributes.

Some further supposed abstract objects that are like attributes, with respect to the identity problem, are the *propositions*—in the sense of entities that somehow correspond to sentences as attributes correspond to predicates. Now if attributes clamor for recognition as objects of the attributary attitudes, so do propositions as objects of the propositional attitudes: believing, wishing, and the rest.[8]

Overwhelmed by the problem of identity of attributes and of propositions, however, one may choose to make a clean sweep of the lot, and undertake to manage the attributary and propositional attitudes somehow without them. Philosophers who take this austere line will perhaps resort to actual linguistic forms, sentences, instead of propositions, as objects of the propositional attitudes; and to actual linguistic forms, predicates, instead of attributes, as objects of the attributary attitudes.

Against such resort to linguistic forms one hears the following objection, due to Church and Langford.[9] If what are believed are mere sentences, then "Edwin believes the English sentence S" goes correctly into German as "Edwin glaubt den englischen Satz S," with S unchanged. But it also goes correctly into German as "Edwin glaubt" followed by a German translation of S in indirect discourse. These two German reports, one quoting the English sentence and the other using German indirect discourse, must then be equivalent. But they are not, it is argued, since a German ignorant of English cannot equate them. Now I am not altogether satisfied with this argument. It rests on the notion of linguistic equivalence, or sameness of meaning; and this has seemed dubious as a tool of philosophical analysis. There is, however, another objection to taking linguistic forms as objects of the attributary and propositional attitudes; viz., simply that that course is discouragingly artificial. With this objection I sympathize.

[8] See my "Quantifiers and propositional attitudes," *Journal of Philosophy* 53 (1956), 177–187.

[9] Alonzo Church, "On Carnap's analysis of statements of assertion and belief," *Analysis* 10 (1950), 97–99. Reprinted in *Philosophy and Analysis* (Margaret Macdonald, ed.), Oxford and New York: Blackwell and Philosophical Library, 1954.

Perhaps, after all, we should be more receptive to the first and least premeditated of the alternatives. We might keep attributes and propositions after all, but just not try to cope with the problem of their individuation. We might deliberately acquiesce in the old unregenerate positing of attributes and propositions without hint of a standard of identity. The precept "No entity without identity" might simply be relaxed. Certainly the positing of first objects makes no sense except as keyed to identity; but those patterns of thing talk, once firmly inculcated, have in fact enabled us to talk of attributes and propositions in partial grammatical analogy, without an accompanying standard of identity for them. Why not just accept them thus, as twilight half-entities to which the identity concept is not to apply? [10] If the disreputability of their origins is undeniable, still bastardy, to the enlightened mind, is no disgrace. This liberal line accords with the Oxford philosophy of ordinary language, much though I should regret, by my sympathetic reference, to cause any twinge of sorrow to my revered predecessor in this presidential chair.

What might properly count against countenancing such half-entities, inaccessible to identity, is a certain disruption of logic. For, if we are to tolerate the half-entities without abdication of philosophical responsibility, we must adjust the logic of our conceptual scheme to receive them, and then weigh any resulting complexity against the benefits of the half-entities in connection with propositional and attributary attitudes and elsewhere.

But I am not sure that even philosophical responsibility requires settling for one all-purpose system.[11] Propositional and

[10] Frege did so in *Grundgesetze der Arithmetik*, where he was at pains not to subject *Begriffe* to identity. See also Peter Geach, "Class and concept," *Philosophical Review* 64 (1955), 561–570.

[11] See James B. Conant, *Modern Science and Modern Man*, New York: Columbia University, 1952, pp. 98 ff.

attributary attitudes belong to daily discourse of hopes, fears, and purposes; causal science gets on well without them. The fact that science has shunned them and fared so well could perhaps encourage a philosopher of sanguine temper to try to include that erstwhile dim domain within an overhauled universal system, science-worthy throughout. But a reasonable if less ambitious alternative would be to keep a relatively simple and austere conceptual scheme, free of half-entities, for official scientific business, and then accommodate the half-entities in a second-grade system.

In any event the idea of accommodating half-entities without identity illustrates how the individuative, object-oriented conceptual scheme so natural to us could conceivably begin to evolve away.

It seemed in our reflections on the child that the category of bulk terms was a survival of a pre-individuative phase. We were thinking ontogenetically, but the phylogenetic parallel is plausible too: we may have in the bulk term a relic, half vestigial and half adapted, of a pre-individuative phase in the evolution of our conceptual scheme. And some day, correspondingly, something of our present individuative talk may in turn end up, half vestigial and half adapted, within a new and as yet unimagined pattern beyond individuation.

Transition to some such radically new pattern could occur either through a conscious philosophical enterprise or by slow and unreasoned development along lines of least resistance. A combination of both factors is likeliest; and anyway the two differ mainly in degree of deliberateness. Our patterns of thought or language have been evolving, under pressure of inherent inadequacies and changing needs, since the dawn of language; and, whether we help guide it or not, we may confidently look forward to more of the same.

Translation of our remote past or future discourse into the terms we now know could be about as tenuous and arbitrary a projection as translation of the heathen language was seen to be. Conversely, even to speak of that remote medium as radically different from ours is, as remarked in the case of the heathen language, to say no more than that the translations do not come smoothly. We have, to be sure, a mode of access to future stages of our own evolution that is denied us in the case of the heathen language: we can sit and evolve. But even those historical gradations, if somehow traced down the ages and used as clues to translation between widely separated evolutionary stages, would still be gradations only, and in no sense clues to fixed ideas beneath the flux of language. For the obstacle to correlating conceptual schemes is not that there is anything ineffable about language or culture, near or remote. The whole truth about the most outlandish linguistic behavior is just as accessible to us, in our current Western conceptual scheme, as are other chapters of zoology. The obstacle is only that any one intercultural correlation of words and phrases, and hence of theories, will be just one among various empirically admissible correlations, whether it is suggested by historical gradations or by unaided analogy; there is nothing for such a correlation to be uniquely right or wrong about. In saying this I philosophize from the vantage point only of our own provincial conceptual scheme and scientific epoch, true; but I know no better.

2

Ontological Relativity

I

I listened to Dewey on Art as Experience when I was a graduate student in the spring of 1931. Dewey was then at Harvard as the first William James Lecturer. I am proud now to be at Columbia as the first John Dewey Lecturer.

Philosophically I am bound to Dewey by the naturalism that dominated his last three decades. With Dewey I hold that knowledge, mind, and meaning are part of the same world that they have to do with, and that they are to be studied in the same empirical spirit that animates natural science. There is no place for a prior philosophy.

When a naturalistic philosopher addresses himself to the philosophy of mind, he is apt to talk of language. Meanings are, first and foremost, meanings of language. Language is a social art which we all acquire on the evidence solely of other people's overt behavior under publicly recognizable circumstances. Meanings, therefore, those very models of mental entities, end up as grist for the behaviorist's mill. Dewey was explicit on the point: "Meaning . . . is not a psychic existence; it is primarily a property of behavior." [1]

Once we appreciate the institution of language in these terms, we see that there cannot be, in any useful sense, a private language. This point was stressed by Dewey in the twenties. "Soliloquy," he wrote, "is the product and reflex of converse with others" (170). Further along he expanded the point thus: "Language is specifically a mode of interaction of at least two beings, a speaker and a hearer; it presupposes an organized group to which these creatures belong, and from whom they have acquired their habits of speech. It is therefore a relationship" (185). Years later, Wittgenstein likewise rejected private language. When Dewey was writing in this naturalistic vein, Wittgenstein still held his copy theory of language.

The copy theory in its various forms stands closer to the main philosophical tradition, and to the attitude of common sense today. Uncritical semantics is the myth of a museum in which the exhibits are meanings and the words are labels. To switch languages is to change the labels. Now the naturalist's primary objection to this view is not an objection to meanings on account of their being mental entities, though that could be objection enough. The primary objection persists even if we take the labeled exhibits not as mental ideas but as Platonic ideas or even as the denoted concrete objects. Semantics is vitiated by a pernicious mentalism as long as we regard a man's semantics as somehow determinate in his mind beyond what might be implicit in his dispositions to overt behavior. It is the very facts about meaning, not the entities meant, that must be construed in terms of behavior.

There are two parts to knowing a word. One part is being

[1] J. Dewey, *Experience and Nature* (La Salle, Ill.: Open Court, 1925, 1958), p. 179.

familiar with the sound of it and being able to reproduce it. This part, the phonetic part, is achieved by observing and imitating other people's behavior, and there are no important illusions about the process. The other part, the semantic part, is knowing how to use the word. This part, even in the paradigm case, is more complex than the phonetic part. The word refers, in the paradigm case, to some visible object. The learner has now not only to learn the word phonetically, by hearing it from another speaker; he also has to see the object; and in addition to this, in order to capture the relevance of the object to the word, he has to see that the speaker also sees the object. Dewey summed up the point thus: "The characteristic theory about B's understanding of A's sounds is that he responds to the thing from the standpoint of A" (178). Each of us, as he learns his language, is a student of his neighbor's behavior; and conversely, insofar as his tries are approved or corrected, he is a subject of his neighbor's behavioral study.

The semantic part of learning a word is more complex than the phonetic part, therefore, even in simple cases: we have to see what is stimulating the other speaker. In the case of words not directly ascribing observable traits to things, the learning process is increasingly complex and obscure; and obscurity is the breeding place of mentalistic semantics. What the naturalist insists on is that, even in the complex and obscure parts of language learning, the learner has no data to work with but the overt behavior of other speakers.

When with Dewey we turn thus toward a naturalistic view of language and a behavioral view of meaning, what we give up is not just the museum figure of speech. We give up an assurance of determinacy. Seen according to the museum myth, the words and sentences of a language have their determinate meanings. To discover the meanings of the native's words we may have to observe his behavior, but still the meanings of the words are supposed to be determinate in the native's *mind*, his mental museum, even in cases where behavioral criteria are powerless to discover them for us. When on the other hand we recognize with Dewey that "meaning . . . is primarily a property of behavior," we recognize that there are no meanings, nor likenesses nor distinctions of meaning, beyond what are implicit in people's dispositions to overt behavior. For naturalism the question whether two expressions are alike or unlike in meaning has no determinate answer, known or unknown, except insofar as the answer is settled in principle by people's speech dispositions, known or unknown. If by these standards there are indeterminate cases, so much the worse for the terminology of meaning and likeness of meaning.

To see what such indeterminacy would be like, suppose there were an expression in a remote language that could be translated into English equally defensibly in either of two ways, unlike in meaning in English. I am not speaking of ambiguity within the native language. I am supposing that one and the same native use of the expression can be given either of the English translations, each being accommodated by compensating adjustments in the translation of other words. Suppose both translations, along with these accommodations in each case, accord equally well with all observable behavior on the part of speakers of the remote language and speakers of English. Suppose they accord perfectly not only with behavior actually observed, but with all dispositions to behavior on the part of all the speakers concerned. On these assumptions it would be forever impossible to know of one of these translations that it was the right one, and the other wrong. Still, if the museum myth were true, there would be a right and wrong of the matter; it is just that we would never know, not having access to the museum. See language naturalistically, on the other hand, and you have to see the notion of likeness of meaning in such a case simply as nonsense.

I have been keeping to the hypothetical. Turning now to examples, let me begin with a disappointing one and work up. In the French construction "ne . . . rien" you can translate "rien" into English as "anything" or as "nothing" at will, and then accommodate your choice by translating "ne" as "not" or by construing it as pleonastic. This example is disappointing because you can object that I have merely cut the French units too small. You can believe the mentalistic myth of the meaning museum and still grant that "rien" of itself has no meaning, being no whole label; it is part of "ne . . . rien," which has its meaning as a whole.

I began with this disappointing example because I think its conspicuous trait—its dependence on cutting language into segments too short to carry meanings—is the secret of the more serious cases as well. What makes other cases more serious is that the segments they involve are seriously long: long enough to be predicates and to be true of things and hence, you would think, to carry meanings.

An artificial example which I have used elsewhere [2] depends on the fact that a whole rabbit is present when and only when an undetached part of a rabbit is present; also when and only when a temporal stage of a rabbit is present. If we are wondering whether to translate a native expression "gavagai" as "rabbit" or as "undetached rabbit part" or as "rabbit stage," we can never settle the matter simply by ostension—that is, simply by

[2] Quine, *Word and Object* (Cambridge, Mass.: MIT Press, 1960), §12.

repeatedly querying the expression "gavagai" for the native's assent or dissent in the presence of assorted stimulations.

Before going on to urge that we cannot settle the matter by non-ostensive means either, let me belabor this ostensive predicament a bit. I am not worrying, as Wittgenstein did, about simple cases of ostension. The color word "sepia," to take one of his examples,[3] can certainly be learned by an ordinary process of conditioning, or induction. One need not even be told that sepia is a color and not a shape or a material or an article. True, barring such hints, many lessons may be needed, so as to eliminate wrong generalizations based on shape, material, etc., rather than color, and so as to eliminate wrong notions as to the intended boundary of an indicated example, and so as to delimit the admissible variations of color itself. Like all conditioning, or induction, the process will depend ultimately also on one's own inborn propensity to find one stimulation qualitatively more akin to a second stimulation than to a third; otherwise there can never be any selective reinforcement and extinction of responses.[4] Still, in principle nothing more is needed in learning "sepia" than in any conditioning or induction.

But the big difference between "rabbit" and "sepia" is that whereas "sepia" is a mass term like "water," "rabbit" is a term of divided reference. As such it cannot be mastered without mastering its principle of individuation: where one rabbit leaves off and another begins. And this cannot be mastered by pure ostension, however persistent.

Such is the quandary over "gavagai": where one gavagai

[3] L. Wittgenstein, *Philosophical Investigations* (New York: Macmillan, 1953), p. 14.
[4] Cf. *Word and Object*, §17.

leaves off and another begins. The only difference between rabbits, undetached rabbit parts, and rabbit stages is in their individuation. If you take the total scattered portion of the spatiotemporal world that is made up of rabbits, and that which is made up of undetached rabbit parts, and that which is made up of rabbit stages, you come out with the same scattered portion of the world each of the three times. The only difference is in how you slice it. And how to slice it is what ostension or simple conditioning, however persistently repeated, cannot teach.

Thus consider specifically the problem of deciding between "rabbit" and "undetached rabbit part" as translation of "gavagai." No word of the native language is known, except that we have settled on some working hypothesis as to what native words or gestures to construe as assent and dissent in response to our pointings and queryings. Now the trouble is that whenever we point to different parts of the rabbit, even sometimes screening the rest of the rabbit, we are pointing also each time to the rabbit. When, conversely, we indicate the whole rabbit with a sweeping gesture, we are still pointing to a multitude of rabbit parts. And note that we do not have even a native analogue of our plural ending to exploit, in asking "gavagai?" It seems clear that no even tentative decision between "rabbit" and "undetached rabbit part" is to be sought at this level.

How would we finally decide? My passing mention of plural endings is part of the answer. Our individuating of terms of divided reference, in English, is bound up with a cluster of interrelated grammatical particles and constructions: plural endings, pronouns, numerals, the "is" of identity, and its adaptations "same" and "other." It is the cluster of interrelated devices in which quantification becomes central when the regimentation of symbolic logic is imposed. If in his language we could ask the native "Is this *gavagai* the same as that one?" while making appropriate multiple ostensions, then indeed we would be well on our way to deciding between "rabbit," "undetached rabbit part," and "rabbit stage." And of course the linguist does at length reach the point where he can ask what purports to be that question. He develops a system for translating our pluralizations, pronouns, numerals, identity, and related devices contextually into the native idiom. He develops such a system by abstraction and hypothesis. He abstracts native particles and constructions from observed native sentences and tries associating these variously with English particles and constructions. Insofar as the native sentences and the thus associated English ones seem to match up in respect of appropriate occasions of use, the linguist feels confirmed in these hypotheses of translation—what I call *analytical hypotheses*.[5]

But it seems that this method, though laudable in practice and the best we can hope for, does not in principle settle the indeterminacy between "rabbit," "undetached rabbit part," and "rabbit stage." For if one workable overall system of analytical hypotheses provides for translating a given native expression into "is the same as," perhaps another equally workable but systematically different system would translate that native expression rather into something like "belongs with." Then when in the native language we try to ask "Is this *gavagai* the same as that?" we could as well be asking "Does this *gavagai* belong with that?" Insofar, the native's assent is no objective evidence for translating "gavagai" as "rabbit" rather than "undetached rabbit part" or "rabbit stage."

This artificial example shares the structure of the trivial earlier example "ne . . . rien." We were able to translate "rien"

---

[5] *Word and Object*, §15. For a summary of the general point of view see also §I of "Speaking of Objects," Chapter 1 in this volume.

as "anything" or as "nothing," thanks to a compensatory adjustment in the handling of "ne." And I suggest that we can translate "gavagai" as "rabbit" or "undetached rabbit part" or "rabbit stage," thanks to compensatory adjustments in the translation of accompanying native locutions. Other adjustments still might accommodate translation of "gavagai" as "rabbithood," or in further ways. I find this plausible because of the broadly structural and contextual character of any considerations that could guide us to native translations of the English cluster of interrelated devices of individuation. There seem bound to be systematically very different choices, all of which do justice to all dispositions to verbal behavior on the part of all concerned.

An actual field linguist would of course be sensible enough to equate "gavagai" with "rabbit," dismissing such perverse alternatives as "undetached rabbit part" and "rabbit stage" out of hand. This sensible choice and others like it would help in turn to determine his subsequent hypotheses as to what native locutions should answer to the English apparatus of individuation, and thus everything would come out all right. The implicit maxim guiding his choice of "rabbit," and similar choices for other native words, is that an enduring and relatively homogeneous object, moving as a whole against a contrasting background, is a likely reference for a short expression. If he were to become conscious of this maxim, he might celebrate it as one of the linguistic universals, or traits of all languages, and he would have no trouble pointing out its psychological plausibility. But he would be wrong; the maxim is his own imposition, toward settling what is objectively indeterminate. It is a very sensible imposition, and I would recommend no other. But I am making a philosophical point.

It is philosophically interesting, moreover, that what is indeterminate in this artificial example is not just meaning, but extension; reference. My remarks on indeterminacy began as a challenge to likeness of meaning. I had us imagining "an expression that could be translated into English equally defensibly in either of two ways, unlike in meaning in English." Certainly likeness of meaning is a dim notion, repeatedly challenged. Of two predicates which are alike in extension, it has never been clear when to say that they are alike in meaning and when not; it is the old matter of featherless bipeds and rational animals, or of equiangular and equilateral triangles. Reference, extension, has been the firm thing; meaning, intension, the infirm. The indeterminacy of translation now confronting us, however, cuts across extension and intension alike. The terms "rabbit," "undetached rabbit part," and "rabbit stage" differ not only in meaning; they are true of different things. Reference itself proves behaviorally inscrutable.

Within the parochial limits of our own language, we can continue as always to find extensional talk clearer than intensional. For the indeterminacy between "rabbit," "rabbit stage," and the rest depended only on a correlative indeterminacy of translation of the English apparatus of individuation—the apparatus of pronouns, pluralization, identity, numerals, and so on. No such indeterminacy obtrudes so long as we think of this apparatus as given and fixed. Given this apparatus, there is no mystery about extension; terms have the same extension when true of the same things. At the level of radical translation, on the other hand, extension itself goes inscrutable.

My example of rabbits and their parts and stages is a contrived example and a perverse one, with which, as I said, the practicing linguist would have no patience. But there are also cases, less bizarre ones, that obtrude in practice. In Japanese there are certain particles, called "classifiers," which may be explained in either of two ways. Commonly they are explained as attaching to numerals, to form compound numerals of distinctive styles. Thus take the numeral for 5. If you attach one classifier to it you get a style of "5" suitable for counting animals; if you attach a different classifier, you get a style of "5" suitable for counting slim things like pencils and chopsticks; and so on. But another way of viewing classifiers is to view them not as constituting part of the numeral, but as constituting part of the term—the term for "chopsticks" or "oxen" or whatever. On this view the classifier does the individuative job that is done in English by "sticks of" as applied to the mass term "wood," or "head of" as applied to the mass term "cattle."

What we have on either view is a Japanese phrase tantamount say to "five oxen," but consisting of three words; [6] the first is in effect the neutral numeral "5," the second is a classifier of the animal kind, and the last corresponds in some fashion to "ox." On one view the neutral numeral and the classifier go together to constitute a declined numeral in the "animal gender," which then modifies "ox" to give, in effect, "five oxen." On the other view the third Japanese word answers not to the individuative term "ox" but to the mass term "cattle"; the classifier applies to this mass term to produce a composite individuative term, in effect "head of cattle"; and the neutral numeral applies directly to all this without benefit of gender, giving "five head of cattle," hence again in effect "five oxen."

If so simple an example is to serve its expository purpose, it needs your connivance. You have to understand "cattle" as a mass term covering only bovines, and "ox" as applying to all bovines. That these usages are not the invariable usages is beside the point. The point is that the Japanese phrase comes out as "five bovines," as desired, when parsed in either of two

---

[6] To keep my account graphic I am counting a certain postpositive particle as a suffix rather than a word.

ways. The one way treats the third Japanese word as an individuative term true of each bovine, and the other way treats
that word rather as a mass term covering the unindividuated
totality of beef on the hoof. These are two very different ways
of treating the third Japanese word; and the three-word phrase
as a whole turns out all right in both cases only because of
compensatory differences in our account of the second word,
the classifier.

This example is reminiscent in a way of our trivial initial example, "ne . . . rien." We were able to represent "rien" as
"anything" or as "nothing," by compensatorily taking "ne" as
negative or as vacuous. We are able now to represent a Japanese word either as an individuative term for bovines or as a
mass term for live beef, by compensatorily taking the classifier
as declining the numeral or as individuating the mass term.
However, the triviality of the one example does not quite carry
over to the other. The early example was dismissed on the
ground that we had cut too small; "rien" was too short for significant translation on its own, and "ne . . . rien" was the
significant unit. But you cannot dismiss the Japanese example
by saying that the third word was too short for significant
translation on its own and that only the whole three-word
phrase, tantamount to "five oxen," was the significant unit. You
cannot take this line unless you are prepared to call a word too
short for significant translation even when it is long enough to
be a term and carry denotation. For the third Japanese word
is, on either approach, a term: on one approach a term of divided reference, and on the other a mass term. If you are indeed prepared thus to call a word too short for significant
translation even when it is a denoting term, then in a back-
handed way you are granting what I wanted to prove: the inscrutability of reference.

Between the two accounts of Japanese classifiers there is no question of right and wrong. The one account makes for more efficient translation into idiomatic English; the other makes for more of a feeling for the Japanese idiom. Both fit all verbal behavior equally well. All whole sentences, and even component phrases like "five oxen," admit of the same net overall English translations on either account. This much is invariant. But what is philosophically interesting is that the reference or extension of shorter terms can fail to be invariant. Whether that third Japanese word is itself true of each ox, or whether on the other hand it is a mass term which needs to be adjoined to the classifier to make a term which is true of each ox—here is a question that remains undecided by the totality of human dispositions to verbal behavior. It is indeterminate in principle; there is no fact of the matter. Either answer can be accommodated by an account of the classifier. Here again, then, is the inscrutability of reference—illustrated this time by a humdrum point of practical translation.

The inscrutability of reference can be brought closer to home by considering the word "alpha," or again the word "green." In our use of these words and others like them there is a systematic ambiguity. Sometimes we use such words as concrete general terms, as when we say the grass is green, or that some inscription begins with an alpha. Sometimes on the other hand we use them as abstract singular terms, as when we say that green is a color and alpha is a letter. Such ambiguity is encouraged by the fact that there is nothing in ostension to distinguish the two uses. The pointing that would be done in teaching the concrete general term "green," or "alpha," differs none from the pointing that would be done in teaching the abstract singular term "green" or "alpha." Yet the objects referred to by the word are very different under the two uses; under the one use the word is true of many concrete objects, and under the other use it names a single abstract object.

We can of course tell the two uses apart by seeing how the word turns up in sentences: whether it takes an indefinite article, whether it takes a plural ending, whether it stands as singular subject, whether it stands as modifier, as predicate complement, and so on. But these criteria appeal to our special English grammatical constructions and particles, our special English apparatus of individuation, which, I already urged, is itself subject to indeterminacy of translation. So, from the point of view of translation into a remote language, the distinction between a concrete general and an abstract singular term is in the same predicament as the distinction between "rabbit," "rabbit part," and "rabbit stage." Here then is another example of the inscrutability of reference, since the difference between the concrete general and the abstract singular is a difference in the objects referred to.

Incidentally we can concede this much indeterminacy also to the "sepia" example, after all. But this move is not evidently what was worrying Wittgenstein.

The ostensive indistinguishability of the abstract singular from the concrete general turns upon what may be called "deferred ostension," as opposed to direct ostension. First let me define direct ostension. The *ostended point,* as I shall call it, is the point where the line of the pointing finger first meets an opaque surface. What characterizes *direct ostension,* then, is that the term which is being ostensively explained is true of something that contains the ostended point. Even such direct ostension has its uncertainties, of course, and these are familiar. There is the question how wide an environment of the ostended point is meant to be covered by the term that is being ostensively explained. There is the question how considerably an absent thing or substance might be allowed to differ from what is now ostended, and still be covered by the term that is now being ostensively explained. Both of these questions can in principle be settled as well as need be by induction from multiple ostensions. Also, if the term is a term of divided reference like "apple," there is the question of individuation: the question where one of its objects leaves off and another begins. This can be settled by induction from multiple ostensions of a more elaborate kind, accompanied by expressions like "same apple" and "another," if an equivalent of this English apparatus of individuation has been settled on; otherwise the indeterminacy persists that was illustrated by "rabbit," "undetached rabbit part," and "rabbit stage."

Such, then, is the way of direct ostension. Other ostension I call *deferred*. It occurs when we point at the gauge, and not the gasoline, to show that there is gasoline. Also it occurs when we explain the abstract singular term "green" or "alpha" by pointing at grass or a Greek inscription. Such pointing is direct ostension when used to explain the concrete general term "green" or "alpha," but it is deferred ostension when used to explain the abstract singular terms; for the abstract object which is the color green or the letter alpha does not contain the ostended point, nor any point.

Deferred ostension occurs very naturally when, as in the case of the gasoline gauge, we have a correspondence in mind. Another such example is afforded by the Gödel numbering of expressions. Thus if 7 has been assigned as Gödel number of the letter alpha, a man conscious of the Gödel numbering would not hesitate to say "Seven" on pointing to an inscription of the Greek letter in question. This is, on the face of it, a doubly deferred ostension: one step of deferment carries us from the inscription to the letter as abstract object, and a second step carries us thence to the number.

By appeal to our apparatus of individuation, if it is available, we can distinguish between the concrete general and the abstract singular use of the word "alpha"; this we saw. By appeal again to that apparatus, and in particular to identity, we can evidently settle also whether the word "alpha" in its abstract singular use is being used really to name the letter or whether, perversely, it is being used to name the Gödel number of the letter. At any rate we can distinguish these alternatives if also we have located the speaker's equivalent of the numeral "7" to our satisfaction; for we can ask him whether alpha *is* 7.

These considerations suggest that deferred ostension adds no essential problem to those presented by direct ostension. Once we have settled upon analytical hypotheses of translation covering identity and the other English particles relating to individuation, we can resolve not only the indecision between "rabbit" and "rabbit stage" and the rest, which came of direct ostension, but also any indecision between concrete general and abstract singular, and any indecision between expression and Gödel number, which come of deferred ostension. However, this conclusion is too sanguine. The inscrutability of reference runs deep, and it persists in a subtle form even if we accept identity and the rest of the apparatus of individuation as fixed and settled; even, indeed, if we forsake radical translation and think only of English.

Consider the case of a thoughtful protosyntactician. He has a formalized system of first-order proof theory, or protosyntax, whose universe comprises just expressions, that is, strings of signs of a specified alphabet. Now just what sorts of things, more specifically, are these expressions? They are types, not tokens. So, one might suppose, each of them is the set of all its tokens. That is, each expression is a set of inscriptions which are variously situated in space-time but are classed together by virtue of a certain similarity in shape. The concatenate $x^\frown y$ of two expressions x and y, in a given order, will be the set of all inscriptions each of which has two parts which are tokens respectively of x and y and follow one upon the other in that order. But $x^\frown y$ may then be the null set, though x and y are not null; for it may be that inscriptions belonging to x and y happen to turn up head to tail nowhere, in the past, present, or future. This danger increases with the lengths of x and y. But it is easily seen to violate a law of protosyntax which says that $x = z$ whenever $x^\frown y = z^\frown y$.

Thus it is that our thoughtful protosyntactician will not construe the things in his universe as sets of inscriptions. He can still take his atoms, the single signs, as sets of inscriptions, for there is no risk of nullity in these cases. And then, instead of taking his strings of signs as sets of inscriptions, he can invoke the mathematical notion of sequence and take them as sequences of signs. A familiar way of taking sequences, in turn, is as a mapping of things on numbers. On this approach an expression or string of signs becomes a finite set of pairs each of which is the pair of a sign and a number.

This account of expressions is more artificial and more complex than one is apt to expect who simply says he is letting his variables range over the strings of such and such signs. Moreover, it is not the inevitable choice; the considerations that motivated it can be met also by alternative constructions. One of these constructions is Gödel numbering itself, and it is temptingly simple. It uses just natural numbers, whereas the foregoing construction used sets of one-letter inscriptions and also natural numbers and sets of pairs of these. How clear is it that at just *this* point we have dropped expressions in favor of numbers? What is clearer is merely that in both constructions we were artificially devising models to satisfy laws that expressions in an unexplicated sense had been meant to satisfy.

So much for expressions. Consider now the arithmetician himself, with his elementary number theory. His universe comprises the natural numbers outright. Is it clearer than the protosyntactician's? What, after all, is a natural number? There are Frege's version, Zermelo's, and von Neumann's, and countless further alternatives, all mutually incompatible and equally correct. What we are doing in any one of these explications of natural number is to devise set-theoretic models to satisfy laws which the natural numbers in an unexplicated sense had been meant to satisfy. The case is quite like that of protosyntax.

It will perhaps be felt that any set-theoretic explication of natural number is at best a case of *obscurum per obscurius;* that all explications must assume something, and the natural numbers themselves are an admirable assumption to start with. I must agree that a construction of sets and set theory from natural numbers and arithmetic would be far more desirable than the familiar opposite. On the other hand our impression of the clarity even of the notion of natural number itself has suffered somewhat from Gödel's proof of the impossibility of a complete proof procedure for elementary number theory, or, for that matter, from Skolem's and Henkin's observations that all laws of natural numbers admit nonstandard models.[7]

We are finding no clear difference between *specifying* a universe of discourse—the range of the variables of quantification —and *reducing* that universe to some other. We saw no significant difference between clarifying the notion of expression and supplanting it by that of number. And now to say more partic-

[7] See Leon Henkin, "Completeness in the theory of types," *Journal of Symbolic Logic* 15 (1950), 81–91, and references therein.

ularly what numbers themselves are is in no evident way different from just dropping numbers and assigning to arithmetic one or another new model, say in set theory.

Expressions are known only by their laws, the laws of concatenation theory, so that any constructs obeying those laws—Gödel numbers, for instance—are *ipso facto* eligible as explications of expression. Numbers in turn are known only by their laws, the laws of arithmetic, so that any constructs obeying those laws—certain sets, for instance—are eligible in turn as explications of number. Sets in turn are known only by their laws, the laws of set theory.

Russell pressed a contrary thesis, long ago. Writing of numbers, he argued that for an understanding of number the laws of arithmetic are not enough; we must know the applications, we must understand numerical discourse embedded in discourse of other matters. In applying number, the key notion, he urged, is *Anzahl:* there are n so-and-sos. However, Russell can be answered. First take, specifically, *Anzahl.* We can define "there are n so-and-sos" without ever deciding what numbers are, apart from their fulfillment of arithmetic. That there are n so-and-sos can be explained simply as meaning that the so-and-sos are in one-to-one correspondence with the numbers up to n.[8]

Russell's more general point about application can be answered too. Always, if the structure is there, the applications will fall into place. As paradigm it is perhaps sufficient to recall again this reflection on expressions and Gödel numbers: that even the pointing out of an inscription is no final evidence that our talk is of expressions and not of Gödel numbers. We can always plead deferred ostension.

[8] For more on this theme see my *Set Theory and Its Logic* (Cambridge, Mass.: Harvard, 1963, 1969), §11.

It is in this sense true to say, as mathematicians often do, that arithmetic is all there is to number. But it would be a confusion to express this point by saying, as is sometimes said, that numbers are any things fulfilling arithmetic. This formulation is wrong because distinct domains of objects yield distinct models of arithmetic. Any progression can be made to serve; and to identify all progressions with one another, e.g., to identify the progression of odd numbers with the progression of evens, would contradict arithmetic after all.

So, though Russell was wrong in suggesting that numbers need more than their arithmetical properties, he was right in objecting to the definition of numbers as any things fulfilling arithmetic. The subtle point is that any progression will serve as a version of number so long and only so long as we stick to one and the same progression. Arithmetic is, in this sense, all there is to number: there is no saying absolutely what the numbers are; there is only arithmetic.[9]

II

I first urged the inscrutability of reference with the help of examples like the one about rabbits and rabbit parts. These used direct ostension, and the inscrutability of reference hinged on the indeterminacy of translation of identity and other individuative apparatus. The setting of these examples, accordingly, was radical translation: translation from a remote language on behavioral evidence, unaided by prior dictionaries. Moving then to deferred ostension and abstract objects, we

[9] Paul Benacerraf, "What numbers cannot be," *Philosophical Review* 74 (1965), 47–73, develops this point. His conclusions differ in some ways from those I shall come to.

found a certain dimness of reference pervading the home language itself.

Now it should be noted that even for the earlier examples the resort to a remote language was not really essential. On deeper reflection, radical translation begins at home. Must we equate our neighbor's English words with the same strings of phonemes in our own mouths? Certainly not; for sometimes we do not thus equate them. Sometimes we find it to be in the interests of communication to recognize that our neighbor's use of some word, such as "cool" or "square" or "hopefully," differs from ours, and so we translate that word of his into a different string of phonemes in our idiolect. Our usual domestic rule of translation is indeed the homophonic one, which simply carries each string of phonemes into itself; but still we are always prepared to temper homophony with what Neil Wilson has called the "principle of charity." [10] We will construe a neighbor's word heterophonically now and again if thereby we see our way to making his message less absurd.

The homophonic rule is a handy one on the whole. That it works so well is no accident, since imitation and feedback are what propagate a language. We acquired a great fund of basic words and phrases in this way, imitating our elders and encouraged by our elders amid external circumstances to which the phrases suitably apply. Homophonic translation is implicit in this social method of learning. Departure from homophonic translation in this quarter would only hinder communication. Then there are the relatively rare instances of opposite kind, due to divergence in dialect or confusion in an individual, where homophonic translation incurs negative feedback. But what tends to escape notice is that there is also a vast mid-

[10] N. L. Wilson, "Substances without substrata," *Review of Metaphysics* 12 (1959), 521–539, p. 532.

region where the homophonic method is indifferent. Here, gratuitously, we can systematically reconstrue our neighbor's apparent references to rabbits as really references to rabbit stages, and his apparent references to formulas as really references to Gödel numbers and vice versa. We can reconcile all this with our neighbor's verbal behavior, by cunningly readjusting our translations of his various connecting predicates so as to compensate for the switch of ontology. In short, we can reproduce the inscrutability of reference at home. It is of no avail to check on this fanciful version of our neighbor's meanings by asking him, say, whether he really means at a certain point to refer to formulas or to their Gödel numbers; for our question and his answer—"By all means, the numbers"—have lost their title to homophonic translation. The problem at home differs none from radical translation ordinarily so called except in the willfulness of this suspension of homophonic translation.

I have urged in defense of the behavioral philosophy of language, Dewey's, that the inscrutability of reference is not the inscrutability of a fact; there is no fact of the matter. But if there is really no fact of the matter, then the inscrutability of reference can be brought even closer to home than the neighbor's case; we can apply it to ourselves. If it is to make sense to say even of oneself that one is referring to rabbits and formulas and not to rabbit stages and Gödel numbers, then it should make sense equally to say it of someone else. After all, as Dewey stressed, there is no private language.

We seem to be maneuvering ourselves into the absurd position that there is no difference on any terms, interlinguistic or intralinguistic, objective or subjective, between referring to rabbits and referring to rabbit parts or stages; or between referring to formulas and referring to their Gödel numbers. Surely this is absurd, for it would imply that there is no difference between the rabbit and each of its parts or stages, and no difference between a formula and its Gödel number. Reference would seem now to become nonsense not just in radical translation but at home.

Toward resolving this quandary, begin by picturing us at home in our language, with all its predicates and auxiliary devices. This vocabulary includes "rabbit," "rabbit part," "rabbit stage," "formula," "number," "ox," "cattle"; also the two-place predicates of identity and difference, and other logical particles. In these terms we can say in so many words that this is a formula and that a number, this a rabbit and that a rabbit part, this and that the same rabbit, and this and that different parts. *In just those words.* This network of terms and predicates and auxiliary devices is, in relativity jargon, our frame of reference, or coordinate system. Relative to *it* we can and do talk meaningfully and distinctively of rabbits and parts, numbers and formulas. Next, as in recent paragraphs, we contemplate alternative denotations for our familiar terms. We begin to appreciate that a grand and ingenious permutation of these denotations, along with compensatory adjustments in the interpretations of the auxiliary particles, might still accommodate all existing speech dispositions. This was the inscrutability of reference, applied to ourselves; and it made nonsense of reference. Fair enough; reference *is* nonsense except relative to a coordinate system. In this principle of relativity lies the resolution of our quandary.

It is meaningless to ask whether, in general, our terms "rabbit," "rabbit part," "number," etc., really refer respectively to rabbits, rabbit parts, numbers, etc., rather than to some ingeniously permuted denotations. It is meaningless to ask this absolutely; we can meaningfully ask it only relative to some background language. When we ask, "Does 'rabbit' really refer to rabbits?" someone can counter with the question: "Refer to rabbits in what sense of 'rabbits'?" thus launching a regress; and we need the background language to regress into. The background language gives the query sense, if only relative sense; sense relative in turn to it, this background language. Querying reference in any more absolute way would be like asking absolute position, or absolute velocity, rather than position or velocity relative to a given frame of reference. Also it is very much like asking whether our neighbor may not systematically see everything upside down, or in complementary color, forever undetectably.

We need a background language, I said, to regress into. Are we involved now in an infinite regress? If questions of reference of the sort we are considering make sense only relative to a background language, then evidently questions of reference for the background language make sense in turn only relative to a further background language. In these terms the situation sounds desperate, but in fact it is little different from questions of position and velocity. When we are given position and velocity relative to a given coordinate system, we can always ask in turn about the placing of origin and orientation of axes of that system of coordinates; and there is no end to the succession of further coordinate systems that could be adduced in answering the successive questions thus generated.

In practice of course we end the regress of coordinate systems by something like pointing. And in practice we end the regress of background languages, in discussions of reference, by acquiescing in our mother tongue and taking its words at face value.

Very well; in the case of position and velocity, in practice, pointing breaks the regress. But what of position and velocity apart from practice? what of the regress then? The answer, of course, is the relational doctrine of space; there is no absolute position or velocity; there are just the relations of coordinate systems to one another, and ultimately of things to one another. And I think that the parallel question regarding denotation calls for a parallel answer, a relational theory of what the objects of theories are. What makes sense is to say not what the objects of a theory are, absolutely speaking, but how one theory of objects is interpretable or reinterpretable in another.

The point is not that bare matter is inscrutable: that things are indistinguishable except by their properties. That point does not need making. The present point is reflected better in the riddle about seeing things upside down, or in complementary colors; for it is that things can be inscrutably switched even while carrying their properties with them. Rabbits differ from rabbit parts and rabbit stages not just as bare matter, after all, but in respect of properties; and formulas differ from numbers in respect of properties. What our present reflections are leading us to appreciate is that the riddle about seeing things upside down, or in complementary colors, should be taken seriously and its moral applied widely. The relativistic thesis to which we have come is this, to repeat: it makes no sense to say what the objects of a theory are, beyond saying how to interpret or reinterpret that theory in another. Suppose we are working within a theory and thus treating of its objects. We do so by using the variables of the theory, whose values those objects are, though there be no ultimate sense in which that universe can have been specified. In the language of the theory there are predicates by which to distinguish portions of this universe from other portions, and these predicates differ from one another purely in the roles they play in the laws of the theory. Within this background theory we can show how some subordinate theory, whose universe is some portion of the background universe, can by a reinterpretation be reduced to another subordinate theory whose universe is some lesser portion. Such talk of subordinate theories and their ontologies *is* meaningful, but only relative to the background theory with its own primitively adopted and ultimately inscrutable ontology.

To talk thus of theories raises a problem of formulation. A theory, it will be said, is a set of fully interpreted sentences. (More particularly, it is a deductively closed set: it includes all its own logical consequences, insofar as they are couched in the same notation.) But if the sentences of a theory are fully interpreted, then in particular the range of values of their variables is settled. How then can there be no sense in saying what the objects of a theory are?

My answer is simply that we cannot require theories to be fully interpreted, except in a relative sense, if anything is to count as a theory. In specifying a theory we must indeed fully specify, in our own words, what sentences are to comprise the theory, and what things are to be taken as values of the variables, and what things are to be taken as satisfying the predicate letters; insofar we do fully interpret the theory, *relative* to our own words and relative to our overall home theory which lies behind them. But this fixes the objects of the described theory only relative to those of the home theory; and these can, at will, be questioned in turn.

One is tempted to conclude simply that meaninglessness sets in when we try to pronounce on everything in our universe; that universal predication takes on sense only when furnished with the background of a wider universe, where the predication is no longer universal. And this is even a familiar doctrine, the doctrine that no proper predicate is true of everything. We have all heard it claimed that a predicate is meaningful only by contrast with what it excludes, and hence that being true of everything would make a predicate meaningless. But surely this doctrine is wrong. Surely self-identity, for instance, is not to be rejected as meaningless. For that matter, any statement of fact at all, however brutally meaningful, can be put artificially into a form in which it pronounces on everything. To say merely of Jones that he sings, for instance, is to say of everything that it is other than Jones or sings. We had better beware of repudiating universal predication, lest we be tricked into repudiating everything there is to say.

Carnap took an intermediate line in his doctrine of universal words, or *Allwörter,* in *The Logical Syntax of Language.* He did treat the predicating of universal words as "quasi-syntactical"—as a predication only by courtesy, and without empirical content. But universal words were for him not just any universally true predicates, like "is other than Jones or sings." They were a special breed of universally true predicates, ones that are universally true by the sheer meanings of their words and no thanks to nature. In his later writing this doctrine of universal words takes the form of a distinction between "internal" questions, in which a theory comes to grips with facts about the world, and "external" questions, in which people come to grips with the relative merits of theories.

Should we look to these distinctions of Carnap's for light on ontological relativity? When we found there was no absolute sense in saying what a theory is about, were we sensing the infactuality of what Carnap calls "external questions"? When we found that saying what a theory is about did make sense against a background theory, were we sensing the factuality of internal questions of the background theory? I see no hope of illumination in this quarter. Carnap's universal words were not just any universally true predicates, but, as I said, a special breed; and what distinguishes this breed is not clear. What I said distinguished them was that they were universally true by sheer meanings and not by nature; but this is a very questionable distinction. Talking of "internal" and "external" is no better.

Ontological relativity is not to be clarified by any distinction between kinds of universal predication—unfactual and factual, external and internal. It is not a question of universal predication. When questions regarding the ontology of a theory are meaningless absolutely, and become meaningful relative to a background theory, this is not in general because the background theory has a wider universe. One is tempted, as I said a little while back, to suppose that it is; but one is then wrong.

What makes ontological questions meaningless when taken absolutely is not universality but circularity. A question of the form "What is an F?" can be answered only by recourse to a further term: "An F is a G." The answer makes only relative sense: sense relative to the uncritical acceptance of "G."

We may picture the vocabulary of a theory as comprising logical signs such as quantifiers and the signs for the truth functions and identity, and in addition descriptive or nonlogical signs, which, typically, are singular terms, or names, and general terms, or predicates. Suppose next that in the statements which comprise the theory, that is, are true according to the theory, we abstract from the meanings of the nonlogical vocabulary and from the range of the variables. We are left with the logical form of the theory, or, as I shall say, the *theory form*. Now we may interpret this theory form anew by picking a new universe for its variables of quantification to range over, and assigning objects from this universe to the names, and choosing subsets of this universe as extensions of the one-place predicates, and so on. Each such interpretation of the theory form is called a model of it, if it makes it come out true. Which of these models is meant in a given actual theory cannot, of course, be guessed from the theory form. The intended references of the names and predicates have to be learned rather by ostension, or else by paraphrase in some antecedently familiar vocabulary. But the first of these two ways has proved inconclusive, since, even apart from indeterminacies of translation affecting identity and other logical vocabulary, there is the problem of deferred ostension. Paraphrase in some antecedently familiar vocabulary, then, is our only recourse; and such is ontological relativity. To question the reference of all the terms of our all-inclusive theory becomes meaningless, simply for want of further terms relative to which to ask or answer the question.

It is thus meaningless within the theory to say which of the various possible models of our theory form is our real or intended model. Yet even here we can make sense still of there being many models. For we might be able to show that for each of the models, however unspecifiable, there is bound to be another which is a permutation or perhaps a diminution of the first.

Suppose for example that our theory is purely numerical. Its objects are just the natural numbers. There is no sense in saying, from within that theory, just which of the various models of number theory is in force. But we can observe even from within the theory that, whatever 0, 1, 2, 3, etc. may be, the theory would still hold true if the 17 of this series were moved into the role of 0, and the 18 moved into the role of 1, and so on.

Ontology is indeed doubly relative. Specifying the universe

of a theory makes sense only relative to some background theory, and only relative to some choice of a manual of translation of the one theory into the other. Commonly of course the background theory will simply be a containing theory, and in this case no question of a manual of translation arises. But this is after all just a degenerate case of translation still—the case where the rule of translation is the homophonic one.

We cannot know what something is without knowing how it is marked off from other things. Identity is thus of a piece with ontology. Accordingly it is involved in the same relativity, as may be readily illustrated. Imagine a fragment of economic theory. Suppose its universe comprises persons, but its predicates are incapable of distinguishing between persons whose incomes are equal. The interpersonal relation of equality of income enjoys, within the theory, the substitutivity property of the identity relation itself; the two relations are indistinguishable. It is only relative to a background theory, in which more can be said of personal identity than equality of income, that we are able even to appreciate the above account of the fragment of economic theory, hinging as the account does on a contrast between persons and incomes.

A usual occasion for ontological talk is reduction, where it is shown how the universe of some theory can by a reinterpretation be dispensed with in favor of some other universe, perhaps a proper part of the first. I have treated elsewhere [11] of the reduction of one ontology to another with help of a *proxy function:* a function mapping the one universe into part or all of the other. For instance, the function "Gödel number of" is a proxy function. The universe of elementary proof theory or

[11] Quine, *The Ways of Paradox* (New York: Random House, 1966), pp. 204 ff.; or see *Journal of Philosophy*, 1964, pp. 214 ff.

protosyntax, which consists of expressions or strings of signs, is mapped by this function into the universe of elementary number theory, which consists of numbers.

The proxy function used in reducing one ontology to another need not, like Gödel numbering, be one-to-one. We might, for instance, be confronted with a theory treating of both expressions and ratios. We would cheerfully reduce all this to the universe of natural numbers, by invoking a proxy function which enumerates the expressions in the Gödel way, and enumerates the ratios by the classical method of short diagonals. This proxy function is not one-to-one, since it assigns the same natural number both to an expression and to a ratio. We would tolerate the resulting artificial convergence between expressions and ratios, simply because the original theory made no capital of the distinction between them; they were so invariably and extravagantly unlike that the identity question did not arise. Formally speaking, the original theory used a two-sorted logic.

For another kind of case where we would not require the proxy function to be one-to-one, consider again the fragment of economic theory lately noted. We would happily reduce its ontology of persons to a less numerous one of incomes. The proxy function would assign to each person his income. It is not one-to-one; distinct persons give way to identical incomes. The reason such a reduction is acceptable is that it merges the images of only such individuals as never had been distinguishable by the predicates of the original theory. Nothing in the old theory is contravened by the new identities.

If on the other hand the theory that we are concerned to reduce or reinterpret is straight protosyntax, or a straight arithmetic of ratios or of real numbers, then a one-to-one proxy function is mandatory. This is because any two elements of such a theory are distinguishable in terms of the theory. This is true even for the real numbers, even though not every real number is uniquely specifiable; any two real numbers x and y are still distinguishable, in that $x < y$ or $y < x$ and never $x < x$. A proxy function that did not preserve the distinctness of the elements of such a theory would fail of its purpose of reinterpretation.

One ontology is *always* reducible to another when we are given a proxy function f that is one-to-one. The essential reasoning is as follows. Where P is any predicate of the old system, its work can be done in the new system by a new predicate which we interpret as true of just the correlates fx of the old objects x that P was true of. Thus suppose we take fx as the Gödel number of x, and as our old system we take a syntactical system in which one of the predicates is "is a segment of." The corresponding predicate of the new or numerical system, then, would be one which amounts, so far as its extension is concerned, to the words "is the Gödel number of a segment of that whose Gödel number is." The numerical predicate would not be given this devious form, of course, but would be rendered as an appropriate purely arithmetical condition.

Our dependence upon a background theory becomes especially evident when we reduce our universe U to another V by appeal to a proxy function. For it is only in a theory with an inclusive universe, embracing U and V, that we can make sense of the proxy function. The function maps U into V and hence needs all the old objects of U as well as their new proxies in V.

The proxy function need not exist as an object in the universe even of the background theory. It may do its work merely as what I have called a "virtual class," [12] and Gödel has

---

[12] Quine, *Set Theory and Its Logic*, §§2 f.

called a "notion." [13] That is to say, all that is required toward a function is an open sentence with two free variables, provided that it is fulfilled by exactly one value of the first variable for each object of the old universe as value of the second variable. But the point is that it is only in the background theory, with its inclusive universe, that we can hope to write such a sentence and have the right values at our disposal for its variables.

If the new objects happen to be among the old, so that V is a subclass of U, then the old theory with universe U can itself sometimes qualify as the background theory in which to describe its own ontological reduction. But we cannot do better than that; we cannot declare our new ontological economies without having recourse to the uneconomical old ontology.

This sounds, perhaps, like a predicament: as if no ontological economy is justifiable unless it is a false economy and the repudiated objects really exist after all. But actually this is wrong; there is no more cause for worry here than there is in *reductio ad absurdum*, where we assume a falsehood that we are out to disprove. If what we want to show is that the universe U is excessive and that only a part exists, or need exist, then we are quite within our rights to assume all of U for the space of the argument. We show thereby that if all of U were needed then not all of U would be needed; and so our ontological reduction is sealed by *reductio ad absurdum*.

Toward further appreciating the bearing of ontological relativity on programs of ontological reduction, it is worth while to reexamine the philosophical bearing of the Löwenheim-Skolem

[13] Kurt Gödel, *The Consistency of the Continuum Hypothesis* (Princeton, N.J.: The University Press, 1940), p. 11.

theorem. I shall use the strong early form of the theorem,[14] which depends on the axiom of choice. It says that if a theory is true and has an indenumerable universe, then all but a denumerable part of that universe is dead wood, in the sense that it can be dropped from the range of the variables without falsifying any sentences.

On the face of it, this theorem declares a reduction of all acceptable theories to denumerable ontologies. Moreover, a denumerable ontology is reducible in turn to an ontology specifically of natural numbers, simply by taking the enumeration as the proxy function, if the enumeration is explicitly at hand. And even if it is not at hand, it exists; thus we can still think of all our objects as natural numbers, and merely reconcile ourselves to not always knowing, numerically, which number an otherwise given object is. May we not thus settle for an all-purpose Pythagorean ontology outright?

Suppose, afterward, someone were to offer us what would formerly have qualified as an ontological reduction—a way of dispensing in future theory with all things of a certain sort S, but still leaving an infinite universe. Now in the new Pythagorean setting his discovery would still retain its essential content, though relinquishing the form of an ontological reduction; it would take the form merely of a move whereby some numerically unspecified numbers were divested of some property of numbers that corresponded to S.

Blanket Pythagoreanism on these terms is unattractive, for it

[14] Thoralf Skolem, "Logisch-kombinatorische Untersuchungen über die Erfüllbarkeit oder Beweisbarkeit mathematischer Sätze nebst einem Theorem über dichte Mengen," *Skrifter utgit av Videnskapsselskapet i Kristiania*, 1919. 37 pp. Translation in Jean van Heijenoort, ed., *From Frege to Gödel: Source Book in the History of Mathematical Logic* (Cambridge, Mass.: Harvard, 1967), pp. 252–263.

merely offers new and obscurer accounts of old moves and old problems. On this score again, then, the relativistic proposition seems reasonable: that there is no absolute sense in speaking of the ontology of a theory. It very creditably brands this Pythagoreanism itself as meaningless. For there is no absolute sense in saying that all the objects of a theory are numbers, or that they are sets, or bodies, or something else; this makes no sense unless relative to some background theory. The relevant predicates—"number," "set," "body," or whatever—would be distinguished from *one another* in the background theory by the roles they play in the laws of that theory.

Elsewhere [11] I urged in answer to such Pythagoreanism that we have no ontological reduction in an interesting sense unless we can specify a proxy function. Now where does the strong Löwenheim-Skolem theorem leave us in this regard? If the background theory assumes the axiom of choice and even provides a notation for a general selector operator, can we in these terms perhaps specify an actual proxy function embodying the Löwenheim-Skolem argument?

The theorem is that all but a denumerable part of an ontology can be dropped and not be missed. One could imagine that the proof proceeds by partitioning the universe into denumerably many equivalence classes of indiscriminable objects, such that all but one member of each equivalence class can be dropped as superfluous; and one would then guess that where the axiom of choice enters the proof is in picking a survivor from each equivalence class. If this were so, then with help of Hilbert's selector notation we could indeed express a proxy function. But in fact the Löwenheim-Skolem proof has another structure. I see in the proof even of the strong Löwenheim-Skolem theorem no reason to suppose that a proxy function can be formulated anywhere that will map an indenumerable ontology, say the real numbers, into a denumerable one.

On the face of it, of course, such a proxy function is out of the question. It would have to be one-to-one, as we saw, to provide distinct images of distinct real numbers; and a one-to-one mapping of an indenumerable domain into a denumerable one is a contradiction. In particular it is easy to show in the Zermelo-Fraenkel system of set theory that such a function would neither exist nor admit even of formulation as a virtual class in the notation of the system.

The discussion of the ontology of a theory can make variously stringent demands upon the background theory in which the discussion is couched. The stringency of these demands varies with what is being said about the ontology of the object theory. We are now in a position to distinguish three such grades of stringency.

The least stringent demand is made when, with no view to reduction, we merely explain what things a theory is about, or what things its terms denote. This amounts to showing how to translate part or all of the object theory into the background theory. It is a matter really of showing how we *propose*, with some arbitrariness, to relate terms of the object theory to terms of the background theory; for we have the inscrutability of reference to allow for. But there is here no requirement that the background theory have a wider universe or a stronger vocabulary than the object theory. The theories could even be identical; this is the case when some terms are clarified by definition on the basis of other terms of the same language.

A more stringent demand was observed in the case where a proxy function is used to reduce an ontology. In this case the background theory needed the unreduced universe. But we saw, by considerations akin to *reductio ad absurdum,* that there was little here to regret.

The third grade of stringency has emerged now in the kind of ontological reduction hinted at by the Löwenheim-Skolem theorem. If a theory has by its own account an indenumerable universe, then even by taking that whole unreduced theory as background theory we cannot hope to produce a proxy function that would be adequate to reducing the ontology to a denumerable one. To find such a proxy function, even just a virtual one, we would need a background theory essentially stronger than the theory we were trying to reduce. This demand cannot, like the second grade of stringency above, be accepted in the spirit of *reductio ad absurdum.* It is a demand that simply discourages any general argument for Pythagoreanism from the Löwenheim-Skolem theorem.

A place where we see a more trivial side of ontological relativity is in the case of a finite universe of named objects. Here there is no occasion for quantification, except as an inessential abbreviation; for we can expand quantifications into finite conjunctions and alternations. Variables thus disappear, and with them the question of a universe of values of variables. And the very distinction between names and other signs lapses in turn, since the mark of a name is its admissibility in positions of variables. Ontology thus is emphatically meaningless for a finite theory of named objects, considered in and of itself. Yet we are now talking meaningfully of such finite ontologies. We are able to do so precisely because we are talking, however vaguely and implicitly, within a broader containing theory. What the objects of the finite theory are, makes sense only as a statement of the background theory in its own referential idiom. The answer to the question depends on the background theory, the finite foreground theory, and, of course, the particular manner in which we choose to translate or embed the one in the other.

Ontology is internally indifferent also, I think, to any theory that is complete and decidable. Where we can always settle truth values mechanically, there is no evident internal reason for interest in the theory of quantifiers nor, therefore, in values of variables. These matters take on significance only as we think of the decidable theory as embedded in a richer background theory in which the variables and their values are serious business.

Ontology may also be said to be internally indifferent even to a theory that is not decidable and does not have a finite universe, if it happens still that each of the infinitely numerous objects of the theory has a name. We can no longer expand quantifications into conjunctions and alternations, barring infinitely long expressions. We can, however, revise our semantical account of the truth conditions of quantification, in such a way as to turn our backs on questions of reference. We can explain universal quantifications as true when true under all substitutions; and correspondingly for existential. Such is the course that has been favored by Leśniewski and by Ruth Marcus.[15] Its nonreferential orientation is seen in the fact that it makes no essential use of namehood. That is, additional quantifications could be explained whose variables are placeholders for words of any syntactical category. *Substitutional* quantification, as I call it, thus brings no way of distinguishing

[15] Ruth B. Marcus, "Modalities and intensional languages," *Synthese* 13 (1961), 303–322. I cannot locate an adequate statement of Stanisław Leśniewski's philosophy of quantification in his writings; I have it from his conversations. E. C. Luschei, in *The Logical Systems of Leśniewski* (Amsterdam: North-Holland, 1962), pp. 108 f, confirms my attribution but still cites no passage. On this version of quantification see further "Existence and Quantification," in this volume.

names from other vocabulary, nor any way of distinguishing between genuinely referential or value-taking variables and other place-holders. Ontology is thus meaningless for a theory whose only quantification is substitutionally construed; meaningless, that is, insofar as the theory is considered in and of itself. The question of its ontology makes sense only relative to some translation of the theory into a background theory in which we use referential quantification. The answer depends on both theories and, again, on the chosen way of translating the one into the other.

A final touch of relativity can in some cases cap this, when we try to distinguish between substitutional and referential quantification. Suppose again a theory with an infinite lot of names, and suppose that, by Gödel numbering or otherwise, we are treating of the theory's notations and proofs within the terms of the theory. If we succeed in showing that every result of substituting a name for the variable in a certain open sentence is true in the theory, but at the same time we disprove the universal quantification of the sentence,[16] then certainly we have shown that the universe of the theory contained some nameless objects. This is a case where an absolute decision can be reached in favor of referential quantification and against substitutional quantification, without ever retreating to a background theory.

But consider now the opposite situation, where there is no such open sentence. Imagine on the contrary that, whenever an open sentence is such that each result of substituting a name in it can be proved, its universal quantification can be

---

[16] Such is the typical way of a numerically insegregative system, misleadingly called "ω-inconsistent." See my *Selected Logic Papers* (New York: Random House, 1966), pp. 118 f, or *Journal of Symbolic Logic*, 1953, pp. 122 f.

proved in the theory too. Under these circumstances we can construe the universe as devoid of nameless objects and hence reconstrue the quantifications as substitutional, but we need not. We could still construe the universe as containing name-less objects. It could just happen that the nameless ones are *inseparable* from the named ones, in this sense: it could happen that all properties of nameless objects that we can express in the notation of the theory are shared by named objects.

We could construe the universe of the theory as containing, e.g., all real numbers. Some of them are nameless, since the real numbers are indenumerable while the names are denu-merable. But it could still happen that the nameless reals are inseparable from the named reals. This would leave us unable within the theory to prove a distinction between referential and substitutional quantification.[17] Every expressible quantifi-cation that is true when referentially construed remains true when substitutionally construed, and vice versa.

We might still make the distinction from the vantage point of a background theory. In it we might specify some real num-ber that was nameless in the object theory; for there are al-ways ways of strengthening a theory so as to name more real numbers, though never all. Further, in the background theory, we might construe the universe of the object theory as exhaust-ing the real numbers. In the background theory we could, in this way, clinch the quantifications in the object theory as ref-erential. But this clinching is doubly relative: it is relative to the background theory and to the interpretation or translation imposed on the object theory from within the background theory.

One might hope that this recourse to a background theory

[17] This possibility was suggested by Saul Kripke.

could often be avoided, even when the nameless reals are inseparable from the named reals in the object theory. One might hope by indirect means to show within the object theory that there are nameless reals. For we might prove within the object theory that the reals are indenumerable and that the names are denumerable and hence that there is no function whose arguments are names and whose values exhaust the real numbers. Since the relation of real numbers to their names would be such a function if each real number had a name, we would seem to have proved within the object theory itself that there are nameless reals and hence that quantification must be taken referentially.

However, this is wrong; there is a loophole. This reasoning would prove only that a relation of all real numbers to their names cannot exist as an entity in the universe of the theory. This reasoning denies no number a name in the notation of the theory, as long as the name relation does not belong to the universe of the theory. And anyway we should know better than to expect such a relation, for it is what causes Berry's and Richard's and related paradoxes.

Some theories can attest to their own nameless objects and so claim referential quantification on their own; other theories have to look to background theories for this service. We saw how a theory might attest to its own nameless objects, namely, by showing that some open sentence became true under all constant substitutions but false under universal quantification. Perhaps this is the only way a theory can claim referential import for its own quantifications. Perhaps, when the nameless objects happen to be inseparable from the named, the quantification used in a theory cannot meaningfully be declared referential except through the medium of a background theory. Yet referential quantification is the key idiom of ontology.

Thus ontology can be multiply relative, multiply meaningless apart from a background theory. Besides being unable to say in absolute terms just what the objects are, we are sometimes unable even to distinguish objectively between referential quantification and a substitutional counterfeit. When we do relativize these matters to a background theory, moreover, the relativization itself has two components: relativity to the choice of background theory and relativity to the choice of how to translate the object theory into the background theory. As for the ontology in turn of the background theory, and even the referentiality of its quantification—these matters can call for a background theory in turn.

There is not always a genuine regress. We saw that, if we are merely clarifying the range of the variables of a theory or the denotations of its terms, and are taking the referentiality of quantification itself for granted, we can commonly use the object theory itself as background theory. We found that when we undertake an ontological reduction, we must accept at least the unreduced theory in order to cite the proxy function; but this we were able cheerfully to accept in the spirit of *reductio ad absurdum* arguments. And now in the end we have found further that if we care to question quantification itself, and settle whether it imports a universe of discourse or turns merely on substitution at the linguistic level, we in some cases have genuinely to regress to a background language endowed with additional resources. We seem to have to do this unless the nameless objects are separable from the named in the object theory.

Regress in ontology is reminiscent of the now familiar regress in the semantics of truth and kindred notions—satisfaction, naming. We know from Tarski's work how the semantics, in this sense, of a theory regularly demands an in some way more inclusive theory. This similarity should perhaps not surprise us, since both ontology and satisfaction are matters of reference. In their elusiveness, at any rate—in their emptiness now and again except relative to a broader background—both truth and ontology may in a suddenly rather clear and even tolerant sense be said to belong to transcendental metaphysics.[18]

Note added in proof. Besides such ontological reduction as is provided by proxy functions (cf. pp. 55–60), there is that which consists simply in dropping objects whose absence will not falsify any truths expressible in the notation. Commonly this sort of deflation can be managed by proxy functions, but R. E. Grandy has shown me that sometimes it cannot. Let us by all means recognize it then as a further kind of reduction. In the background language we must, of course, be able to say what class of objects is dropped, just as in other cases we had to be able to specify the proxy function. This requirement seems sufficient still to stem any resurgence of Pythagoreanism on the strength of the Löwenheim-Skolem theorem.

[18] In developing these thoughts I have been helped by discussions with Saul Kripke, Thomas Nagel, and especially Burton Dreben.

3

Epistemology
Naturalized

Epistemology is concerned with the foundations of science. Conceived thus broadly, epistemology includes the study of the foundations of mathematics as one of its departments. Specialists at the turn of the century thought that their efforts in this particular department were achieving notable success: mathematics seemed to reduce altogether to logic. In a more recent perspective this reduction is seen to be better describable as a reduction to logic and set theory. This correction is a disappointment epistemologically, since the firmness and obviousness that we associate with logic cannot be claimed for set theory. But still the success achieved in the foundations of mathematics remains exemplary by comparative standards, and we can illuminate the rest of epistemology somewhat by drawing parallels to this department.

Studies in the foundations of mathematics divide symmetrically into two sorts, conceptual and doctrinal. The conceptual studies are concerned with meaning, the doctrinal with truth. The conceptual studies are concerned with clarifying concepts by defining them, some in terms of others. The doctrinal studies are concerned with establishing laws by proving them, some on the basis of others. Ideally the obscurer concepts would be defined in terms of the clearer ones so as to maximize clarity, and the less obvious laws would be proved from the more obvious ones so as to maximize certainty. Ideally the definitions would generate all the concepts from clear and distinct ideas, and the proofs would generate all the theorems from self-evident truths.

The two ideals are linked. For, if you define all the concepts by use of some favored subset of them, you thereby show how to translate all theorems into these favored terms. The clearer these terms are, the likelier it is that the truths couched in them will be obviously true, or derivable from obvious truths. If in particular the concepts of mathematics were all reducible to the clear terms of logic, then all the truths of mathematics would go over into truths of logic; and surely the truths of logic are all obvious or at least potentially obvious, i.e., derivable from obvious truths by individually obvious steps.

This particular outcome is in fact denied us, however, since mathematics reduces only to set theory and not to logic proper. Such reduction still enhances clarity, but only because of the interrelations that emerge and not because the end terms of the analysis are clearer than others. As for the end truths, the axioms of set theory, these have less obviousness and certainty to recommend them than do most of the mathematical theorems that we would derive from them. Moreover, we know from Gödel's work that no consistent axiom system can cover mathematics even when we renounce self-evidence. Reduction in the foundations of mathematics remains mathematically and philosophically fascinating, but it does not do what the epistemologist would like of it: it does not reveal the ground of mathematical knowledge, it does not show how mathematical certainty is possible.

Still there remains a helpful thought, regarding epistemology generally, in that duality of structure which was especially conspicuous in the foundations of mathematics. I refer to the bifurcation into a theory of concepts, or meaning, and a theory of doctrine, or truth; for this applies to the epistemology of natural knowledge no less than to the foundations of mathematics. The parallel is as follows. Just as mathematics is to be reduced to logic, or logic and set theory, so natural knowledge is to be based somehow on sense experience. This means explaining the notion of body in sensory terms; here is the conceptual side. And it means justifying our knowledge of truths of nature in sensory terms; here is the doctrinal side of the bifurcation.

Hume pondered the epistemology of natural knowledge on both sides of the bifurcation, the conceptual and the doctrinal. His handling of the conceptual side of the problem, the explanation of body in sensory terms, was bold and simple: he identified bodies outright with the sense impressions. If common sense distinguishes between the material apple and our sense impressions of it on the ground that the apple is one and enduring while the impressions are many and fleeting, then, Hume held, so much the worse for common sense; the notion of its being the same apple on one occasion and another is a vulgar confusion.

Nearly a century after Hume's *Treatise*, the same view of bodies was espoused by the early American philosopher Alexander Bryan Johnson.[1] "The word iron names an associated sight and feel," Johnson wrote.

What then of the doctrinal side, the justification of our knowledge of truths about nature? Here, Hume despaired. By

[1] A. B. Johnson, *A Treatise on Language* (New York, 1836; Berkeley, 1947).

his identification of bodies with impressions he did succeed in construing some singular statements about bodies as indubitable truths, yes; as truths about impressions, directly known. But general statements, also singular statements about the future, gained no increment of certainty by being construed as about impressions.

On the doctrinal side, I do not see that we are farther along today than where Hume left us. The Humean predicament is the human predicament. But on the conceptual side there has been progress. There the crucial step forward was made already before Alexander Bryan Johnson's day, although Johnson did not emulate it. It was made by Bentham in his theory of fictions. Bentham's step was the recognition of contextual definition, or what he called paraphrasis. He recognized that to explain a term we do not need to specify an object for it to refer to, nor even specify a synonymous word or phrase; we need only show, by whatever means, how to translate all the whole sentences in which the term is to be used. Hume's and Johnson's desperate measure of identifying bodies with impressions ceased to be the only conceivable way of making sense of talk of bodies, even granted that impressions were the only reality. One could undertake to explain talk of bodies in terms of talk of impressions by translating one's whole sentences about bodies into whole sentences about impressions, without equating the bodies themselves to anything at all.

This idea of contextual definition, or recognition of the sentence as the primary vehicle of meaning, was indispensable to the ensuing developments in the foundations of mathematics. It was explicit in Frege, and it attained its full flower in Russell's doctrine of singular descriptions as incomplete symbols.

Contextual definition was one of two resorts that could be expected to have a liberating effect upon the conceptual side of the epistemology of natural knowledge. The other is resort to the resources of set theory as auxiliary concepts. The epistemologist who is willing to eke out his austere ontology of sense impressions with these set-theoretic auxiliaries is suddenly rich: he has not just his impressions to play with, but sets of them, and sets of sets, and so on up. Constructions in the foundations of mathematics have shown that such set-theoretic aids are a powerful addition; after all, the entire glossary of concepts of classical mathematics is constructible from them. Thus equipped, our epistemologist may not need either to identify bodies with impressions or to settle for contextual definition; he may hope to find in some subtle construction of sets upon sets of sense impressions a category of objects enjoying just the formula properties that he wants for bodies.

The two resorts are very unequal in epistemological status. Contextual definition is unassailable. Sentences that have been given meaning as wholes are undeniably meaningful, and the use they make of their component terms is therefore meaningful, regardless of whether any translations are offered for those terms in isolation. Surely Hume and A. B. Johnson would have used contextual definition with pleasure if they had thought of it. Recourse to sets, on the other hand, is a drastic ontological move, a retreat from the austere ontology of impressions. There are philosophers who would rather settle for bodies outright than accept all these sets, which amount, after all, to the whole abstract ontology of mathematics.

This issue has not always been clear, however, owing to deceptive hints of continuity between elementary logic and set theory. This is why mathematics was once believed to reduce to logic, that is, to an innocent and unquestionable logic, and to inherit these qualities. And this is probably why Russell was content to resort to sets as well as to contextual definition when in *Our Knowledge of the External World* and elsewhere he addressed himself to the epistemology of natural knowledge, on its conceptual side.

To account for the external world as a logical construct of sense data—such, in Russell's terms, was the program. It was Carnap, in his *Der logische Aufbau der Welt* of 1928, who came nearest to executing it.

This was the conceptual side of epistemology; what of the doctrinal? There the Humean predicament remained unaltered. Carnap's constructions, if carried successfully to completion, would have enabled us to translate all sentences about the world into terms of sense data, or observation, plus logic and set theory. But the mere fact that a sentence is *couched* in terms of observation, logic, and set theory does not mean that it can be *proved* from observation sentences by logic and set theory. The most modest of generalizations about observable traits will cover more cases than its utterer can have had occasion actually to observe. The hopelessness of grounding natural science upon immediate experience in a firmly logical way was acknowledged. The Cartesian quest for certainty had been the remote motivation of epistemology, both on its conceptual and its doctrinal side; but that quest was seen as a lost cause. To endow the truths of nature with the full authority of immediate experience was as forlorn a hope as hoping to endow the truths of mathematics with the potential obviousness of elementary logic.

What then could have motivated Carnap's heroic efforts on the conceptual side of epistemology, when hope of certainty on the doctrinal side was abandoned? There were two good reasons still. One was that such constructions could be expected to elicit and clarify the sensory evidence for science, even if the inferential steps between sensory evidence and scientific doctrine must fall short of certainty. The other reason was that such constructions would deepen our understanding of our discourse about the world, even apart from questions of evidence; it would make all cognitive discourse as clear as observation terms and logic and, I must regretfully add, set theory.

It was sad for epistemologists, Hume and others, to have to acquiesce in the impossibility of strictly deriving the science of the external world from sensory evidence. Two cardinal tenets of empiricism remained unassailable, however, and so remain to this day. One is that whatever evidence there *is* for science *is* sensory evidence. The other, to which I shall recur, is that all inculcation of meanings of words must rest ultimately on sensory evidence. Hence the continuing attractiveness of the idea of a *logischer Aufbau* in which the sensory content of discourse would stand forth explicitly.

If Carnap had successfully carried such a construction through, how could he have told whether it was the right one? The question would have had no point. He was seeking what he called a *rational reconstruction*. Any construction of physicalistic discourse in terms of sense experience, logic, and set theory would have been seen as satisfactory if it made the physicalistic discourse come out right. If there is one way there are many, but any would be a great achievement.

But why all this creative reconstruction, all this make-believe? The stimulation of his sensory receptors is all the evidence anybody has had to go on, ultimately, in arriving at his picture of the world. Why not just see how this construction really proceeds? Why not settle for psychology? Such a surrender of the epistemological burden to psychology is a move that was disallowed in earlier times as circular reasoning. If the epistemologist's goal is validation of the grounds of empirical science, he defeats his purpose by using psychology or other empirical science in the validation. However, such scruples against circularity have little point once we have stopped dreaming of deducing science from observations. If we are out simply to understand the link between observation and science, we are well advised to use any available information, including that provided by the very science whose link with observation we are seeking to understand.

But there remains a different reason, unconnected with fears of circularity, for still favoring creative reconstruction. We should like to be able to *translate* science into logic and observation terms and set theory. This would be a great epistemological achievement, for it would show all the rest of the concepts of science to be theoretically superfluous. It would legitimize them—to whatever degree the concepts of set theory, logic, and observation are themselves legitimate—by showing that everything done with the one apparatus could in principle be done with the other. If psychology itself could deliver a truly translational reduction of this kind, we should welcome it; but certainly it cannot, for certainly we did not grow up learning definitions of physicalistic language in terms of a prior language of set theory, logic, and observation. Here, then, would be good reason for persisting in a rational reconstruction: we want to establish the essential innocence of physical concepts, by showing them to be theoretically dispensable.

The fact is, though, that the construction which Carnap outlined in *Der logische Aufbau der Welt* does not give translational reduction either. It would not even if the outline were filled in. The crucial point comes where Carnap is explaining how to assign sense qualities to positions in physical space and time. These assignments are to be made in such a way as to fulfill, as well as possible, certain desiderata which he states, and with growth of experience the assignments are to be revised to suit. This plan, however illuminating, does not offer any key to *translating* the sentences of science into terms of observation, logic, and set theory.

We must despair of any such reduction. Carnap had despaired of it by 1936, when, in "Testability and meaning," [2] he introduced so-called *reduction forms* of a type weaker than definition. Definitions had shown always how to translate sentences into equivalent sentences. Contextual definition of a term showed how to translate sentences containing the term into equivalent sentences lacking the term. Reduction forms of Carnap's liberalized kind, on the other hand, do not in general give equivalences; they give implications. They explain a new term, if only partially, by specifying some sentences which are implied by sentences containing the term, and other sentences which imply sentences containing the term.

It is tempting to suppose that the countenancing of reduction forms in this liberal sense is just one further step of liberalization comparable to the earlier one, taken by Bentham, of countenancing contextual definition. The former and sterner kind of rational reconstruction might have been represented as a fictitious history in which we imagined our ancestors introducing the terms of physicalistic discourse on a phenomenalistic and set-theoretic basis by a succession of contextual definitions. The new and more liberal kind of rational reconstruction is a fictitious history in which we imagine our ancestors introducing those terms by a succession rather of reduction forms of the weaker sort.

This, however, is a wrong comparison. The fact is rather that the former and sterner kind of rational reconstruction, where definition reigned, embodied no fictitious history at all. It was nothing more nor less than a set of directions—or would have

[2] *Philosophy of Science* 3 (1936), 419–471; 4 (1937), 1–40.

been, if successful—for accomplishing everything in terms of phenomena and set theory that we now accomplish in terms of bodies. It would have been a true reduction by translation, a legitimation by elimination. *Definire est eliminare.* Rational reconstruction by Carnap's later and looser reduction forms does none of this.

To relax the demand for definition, and settle for a kind of reduction that does not eliminate, is to renounce the last remaining advantage that we supposed rational reconstruction to have over straight psychology; namely, the advantage of translational reduction. If all we hope for is a reconstruction that links science to experience in explicit ways short of translation, then it would seem more sensible to settle for psychology. Better to discover how science is in fact developed and learned than to fabricate a fictitious structure to a similar effect.

The empiricist made one major concession when he despaired of deducing the truths of nature from sensory evidence. In despairing now even of translating those truths into terms of observation and logico-mathematical auxiliaries, he makes another major concession. For suppose we hold, with the old empiricist Peirce, that the very meaning of a statement consists in the difference its truth would make to possible experience. Might we not formulate, in a chapter-length sentence in observational language, all the difference that the truth of a given statement might make to experience, and might we not then take all this as the translation? Even if the difference that the truth of the statement would make to experience ramifies indefinitely, we might still hope to embrace it all in the logical implications of our chapter-length formulation, just as we can axiomatize an infinity of theorems. In giving up hope of such translation, then, the empiricist is conceding that the empirical meanings of typical statements about the external world are inaccessible and ineffable.

How is this inaccessibility to be explained? Simply on the ground that the experiential implications of a typical statement about bodies are too complex for finite axiomatization, however lengthy? No; I have a different explanation. It is that the typical statement about bodies has no fund of experiential implications it can call its own. A substantial mass of theory, taken together, will commonly have experiential implications; this is how we make verifiable predictions. We may not be able to explain why we arrive at theories which make successful predictions, but we do arrive at such theories.

Sometimes also an experience implied by a theory fails to come off; and then, ideally, we declare the theory false. But the failure falsifies only a block of theory as a whole, a conjunction of many statements. The failure shows that one or more of those statements is false, but it does not show which. The predicted experiences, true and false, are not implied by any one of the component statements of the theory rather than another. The component statements simply do not have empirical meanings, by Peirce's standard; but a sufficiently inclusive portion of theory does. If we can aspire to a sort of *logischer Aufbau der Welt* at all, it must be to one in which the texts slated for translation into observational and logico-mathematical terms are mostly broad theories taken as wholes, rather than just terms or short sentences. The translation of a theory would be a ponderous axiomatization of all the experiential difference that the truth of the theory would make. It would be a queer translation, for it would translate the whole but none of the parts. We might better speak in such a case not of translation but simply of observational evidence for theories;

and we may, following Peirce, still fairly call this the empirical meaning of the theories.

These considerations raise a philosophical question even about ordinary unphilosophical translation, such as from English into Arunta or Chinese. For, if the English sentences of a theory have their meaning only together as a body, then we can justify their translation into Arunta only together as a body. There will be no justification for pairing off the component English sentences with component Arunta sentences, except as these correlations make the translation of the theory as a whole come out right. Any translations of the English sentences into Arunta sentences will be as correct as any other, so long as the net empirical implications of the theory as a whole are preserved in translation. But it is to be expected that many different ways of translating the component sentences, essentially different individually, would deliver the same empirical implications for the theory as a whole; deviations in the translation of one component sentence could be compensated for in the translation of another component sentence. Insofar, there can be no ground for saying which of two glaringly unlike translations of individual sentences is right. [3]

For an uncritical mentalist, no such indeterminacy threatens. Every term and every sentence is a label attached to an idea, simple or complex, which is stored in the mind. When on the other hand we take a verification theory of meaning seriously, the indeterminacy would appear to be inescapable. The Vienna Circle espoused a verification theory of meaning but did not take it seriously enough. If we recognize with Peirce that the meaning of a sentence turns purely on what would count as evidence for its truth, and if we recognize with Duhem that theoretical sentences have their evidence not as

[3] See above, p. 2 ff.

single sentences but only as larger blocks of theory, then the indeterminacy of translation of theoretical sentences is the natural conclusion. And most sentences, apart from observation sentences, are theoretical. This conclusion, conversely, once it is embraced, seals the fate of any general notion of propositional meaning or, for that matter, state of affairs.

Should the unwelcomeness of the conclusion persuade us to abandon the verification theory of meaning? Certainly not. The sort of meaning that is basic to translation, and to the learning of one's own language, is necessarily empirical meaning and nothing more. A child learns his first words and sentences by hearing and using them in the presence of appropriate stimuli. These must be external stimuli, for they must act both on the child and on the speaker from whom he is learning.[4] Language is socially inculcated and controlled; the inculcation and control turn strictly on the keying of sentences to shared stimulation. Internal factors may vary *ad libitum* without prejudice to communication as long as the keying of language to external stimuli is undisturbed. Surely one has no choice but to be an empiricist so far as one's theory of linguistic meaning is concerned.

What I have said of infant learning applies equally to the linguist's learning of a new language in the field. If the linguist does not lean on related languages for which there are previously accepted translation practices, then obviously he has no data but the concomitances of native utterance and observable stimulus situation. No wonder there is indeterminacy of translation—for of course only a small fraction of our utterances report concurrent external stimulation. Granted, the linguist will end up with unequivocal translations of everything; but only by making many arbitrary choices—arbitrary even though un-

[4] See above, p. 28.

conscious—along the way. Arbitrary? By this I mean that different choices could still have made everything come out right that is susceptible in principle to any kind of check.

Let me link up, in a different order, some of the points I have made. The crucial consideration behind my argument for the indeterminacy of translation was that a statement about the world does not always or usually have a separable fund of empirical consequences that it can call its own. That consideration served also to account for the impossibility of an epistemological reduction of the sort where every sentence is equated to a sentence in observational and logico-mathematical terms. And the impossibility of that sort of epistemological reduction dissipated the last advantage that rational reconstruction seemed to have over psychology.

Philosophers have rightly despaired of translating everything into observational and logico-mathematical terms. They have despaired of this even when they have not recognized, as the reason for this irreducibility, that the statements largely do not have their private bundles of empirical consequences. And some philosophers have seen in this irreducibility the bankruptcy of epistemology. Carnap and the other logical positivists of the Vienna Circle had already pressed the term "metaphysics" into pejorative use, as connoting meaninglessness; and the term "epistemology" was next. Wittgenstein and his followers, mainly at Oxford, found a residual philosophical vocation in therapy: in curing philosophers of the delusion that there were epistemological problems.

But I think that at this point it may be more useful to say rather that epistemology still goes on, though in a new setting and a clarified status. Epistemology, or something like it, simply falls into place as a chapter of psychology and hence of natural science. It studies a natural phenomenon, viz., a physical human subject. This human subject is accorded a certain experimentally controlled input—certain patterns of irradiation in assorted frequencies, for instance—and in the fullness of time the subject delivers as output a description of the three-dimensional external world and its history. The relation between the meager input and the torrential output is a relation that we are prompted to study for somewhat the same reasons that always prompted epistemology; namely, in order to see how evidence relates to theory, and in what ways one's theory of nature transcends any available evidence.

Such a study could still include, even, something like the old rational reconstruction, to whatever degree such reconstruction is practicable; for imaginative constructions can afford hints of actual psychological processes, in much the way that mechanical simulations can. But a conspicuous difference between old epistemology and the epistemological enterprise in this new psychological setting is that we can now make free use of empirical psychology.

The old epistemology aspired to contain, in a sense, natural science; it would construct it somehow from sense data. Epistemology in its new setting, conversely, is contained in natural science, as a chapter of psychology. But the old containment remains valid too, in its way. We are studying how the human subject of our study posits bodies and projects his physics from his data, and we appreciate that our position in the world is just like his. Our very epistemological enterprise, therefore, and the psychology wherein it is a component chapter, and the whole of natural science wherein psychology is a component book—all this is our own construction or projection from stimulations like those we were meting out to our epistemological subject. There is thus reciprocal containment, though containment in different senses: epistemology in natural science and natural science in epistemology.

This interplay is reminiscent again of the old threat of circularity, but it is all right now that we have stopped dreaming of deducing science from sense data. We are after an understanding of science as an institution or process in the world, and we do not intend that understanding to be any better than the science which is its object. This attitude is indeed one that Neurath was already urging in Vienna Circle days, with his parable of the mariner who has to rebuild his boat while staying afloat in it.

One effect of seeing epistemology in a psychological setting is that it resolves a stubborn old enigma of epistemological priority. Our retinas are irradiated in two dimensions, yet we see things as three-dimensional without conscious inference. Which is to count as observation—the unconscious two-dimensional reception or the conscious three-dimensional apprehension? In the old epistemological context the conscious form had priority, for we were out to justify our knowledge of the external world by rational reconstruction, and that demands awareness. Awareness ceased to be demanded when we gave up trying to justify our knowledge of the external world by rational reconstruction. What to count as observation now can be settled in terms of the stimulation of sensory receptors, let consciousness fall where it may.

The Gestalt psychologists' challenge to sensory atomism, which seemed so relevant to epistemology forty years ago, is likewise deactivated. Regardless of whether sensory atoms or Gestalten are what favor the forefront of our consciousness, it is simply the stimulations of our sensory receptors that are best looked upon as the input to our cognitive mechanism. Old paradoxes about unconscious data and inference, old problems about chains of inference that would have to be completed too quickly—these no longer matter.

In the old anti-psychologistic days the question of epistemological priority was moot. What is epistemologically prior to what? Are Gestalten prior to sensory atoms because they are noticed, or should we favor sensory atoms on some more subtle ground? Now that we are permitted to appeal to physical stimulation, the problem dissolves; A is epistemologically prior to B if A is causally nearer than B to the sensory receptors. Or, what is in some ways better, just talk explicitly in terms of causal proximity to sensory receptors and drop the talk of epistemological priority.

Around 1932 there was debate in the Vienna Circle over what to count as observation sentences, or *Protokollsätze*.[5] One position was that they had the form of reports of sense impressions. Another was that they were statements of an elementary sort about the external world, e.g., "A red cube is standing on the table." Another, Neurath's, was that they had the form of reports of relations between percipients and external things: "Otto now sees a red cube on the table." The worst of it was that there seemed to be no objective way of settling the matter: no way of making real sense of the question.

Let us now try to view the matter unreservedly in the context of the external world. Vaguely speaking, what we want of observation sentences is that they be the ones in closest causal proximity to the sensory receptors. But how is such proximity to be gauged? The idea may be rephrased this way: observation sentences are sentences which, as we learn language, are most strongly conditioned to concurrent sensory stimulation rather than to stored collateral information. Thus let us imagine a sentence queried for our verdict as to whether it is true or false; queried for our assent or dissent. Then the sentence is an observation sentence if our verdict depends only on the sensory stimulation present at the time.

But a verdict cannot depend on present stimulation to the exclusion of stored information. The very fact of our having

---

[5] Carnap and Neurath in *Erkenntnis* 3 (1932), 204–228.

learned the language evinces much storing of information, and of information without which we should be in no position to give verdicts on sentences however observational. Evidently then we must relax our definition of observation sentence to read thus: a sentence is an observation sentence if all verdicts on it depend on present sensory stimulation and on no stored information beyond what goes into understanding the sentence.

This formulation raises another problem: how are we to distinguish between information that goes into understanding a sentence and information that goes beyond? This is the problem of distinguishing between analytic truth, which issues from the mere meanings of words, and synthetic truth, which depends on more than meanings. Now I have long maintained that this distinction is illusory. There is one step toward such a distinction, however, which does make sense: a sentence that is true by mere meanings of words should be expected, at least if it is simple, to be subscribed to by all fluent speakers in the community. Perhaps the controversial notion of analyticity can be dispensed with, in our definition of observation sentence, in favor of this straightforward attribute of community-wide acceptance.

This attribute is of course no explication of analyticity. The community would agree that there have been black dogs, yet none who talk of analyticity would call this analytic. My rejection of the analyticity notion just means drawing no line between what goes into the mere understanding of the sentences of a language and what else the community sees eye-to-eye on. I doubt that an objective distinction can be made between meaning and such collateral information as is community-wide.

Turning back then to our task of defining observation sentences, we get this: an observation sentence is one on which all speakers of the language give the same verdict when given the same concurrent stimulation. To put the point negatively, an observation sentence is one that is not sensitive to differences in past experience within the speech community.

This formulation accords perfectly with the traditional role of the observation sentence as the court of appeal of scientific theories. For by our definition the observation sentences are the sentences on which all members of the community will agree under uniform stimulation. And what is the criterion of membership in the same community? Simply general fluency of dialogue. This criterion admits of degrees, and indeed we may usefully take the community more narrowly for some studies than for others. What count as observation sentences for a community of specialists would not always so count for a larger community.

There is generally no subjectivity in the phrasing of observation sentences, as we are now conceiving them; they will usually be about bodies. Since the distinguishing trait of an observation sentence is intersubjective agreement under agreeing stimulation, a corporeal subject matter is likelier than not.

The old tendency to associate observation sentences with a subjective sensory subject matter is rather an irony when we reflect that observation sentences are also meant to be the intersubjective tribunal of scientific hypotheses. The old tendency was due to the drive to base science on something firmer and prior in the subject's experience; but we dropped that project.

The dislodging of epistemology from its old status of first philosophy loosed a wave, we saw, of epistemological nihilism. This mood is reflected somewhat in the tendency of Polányi, Kuhn, and the late Russell Hanson to belittle the role of evidence and to accentuate cultural relativism. Hanson ventured even to discredit the idea of observation, arguing that so-called observations vary from observer to observer with the amount of knowledge that the observers bring with them. The veteran physicist looks at some apparatus and sees an x-ray tube. The neophyte, looking at the same place, observes rather "a glass and metal instrument replete with wires, reflectors, screws, lamps, and pushbuttons." [6] One man's observation is another man's closed book or flight of fancy. The notion of observation as the impartial and objective source of evidence for science is bankrupt. Now my answer to the x-ray example was already hinted a little while back: what counts as an observation sentence varies with the width of community considered. But we can also always get an absolute standard by taking in all speakers of the language, or most. [7] It is ironical that philosophers, finding the old epistemology untenable as a whole, should react by repudiating a part which has only now moved into clear focus.

Clarification of the notion of observation sentence is a good thing, for the notion is fundamental in two connections. These two correspond to the duality that I remarked upon early in this lecture: the duality between concept and doctrine, between knowing what a sentence means and knowing whether it is true. The observation sentence is basic to both enterprises. Its relation to doctrine, to our knowledge of what is true, is very much the traditional one: observation sentences are the repository of evidence for scientific hypotheses. Its relation to

[6] N. R. Hanson, "Observation and interpretation," in S. Morgenbesser, ed., *Philosophy of Science Today* (New York: Basic Books, 1966).

[7] This qualification allows for occasional deviants such as the insane or the blind. Alternatively, such cases might be excluded by adjusting the level of fluency of dialogue whereby we define sameness of language. (For prompting this note and influencing the development of this paper also in more substantial ways I am indebted to Burton Dreben.)

meaning is fundamental too, since observation sentences are the ones we are in a position to learn to understand first, both as children and as field linguists. For observation sentences are precisely the ones that we can correlate with observable circumstances of the occasion of utterance or assent, independently of variations in the past histories of individual informants. They afford the only entry to a language.

The observation sentence is the cornerstone of semantics. For it is, as we just saw, fundamental to the learning of meaning. Also, it is where meaning is firmest. Sentences higher up in theories have no empirical consequences they can call their own; they confront the tribunal of sensory evidence only in more or less inclusive aggregates. The observation sentence, situated at the sensory periphery of the body scientific, is the minimal verifiable aggregate; it has an empirical content all its own and wears it on its sleeve.

The predicament of the indeterminacy of translation has little bearing on observation sentences. The equating of an observation sentence of our language to an observation sentence of another language is mostly a matter of empirical generalization; it is a matter of identity between the range of stimulations that would prompt assent to the one sentence and the range of stimulations that would prompt assent to the other.[8]

It is no shock to the preconceptions of old Vienna to say that epistemology now becomes semantics. For epistemology remains centered as always on evidence, and meaning remains centered as always on verification; and evidence is verification. What is likelier to shock preconceptions is that meaning, once we get beyond observation sentences, ceases in general to have any clear applicability to single sentences; also that epistemol-

[8] Cf. Quine, *Word and Object*, pp. 31–46, 68.

ogy merges with psychology, as well as with linguistics.

This rubbing out of boundaries could contribute to progress, it seems to me, in philosophically interesting inquiries of a scientific nature. One possible area is perceptual norms. Consider, to begin with, the linguistic phenomenon of phonemes. We form the habit, in hearing the myriad variations of spoken sounds, of treating each as an approximation to one or another of a limited number of norms—around thirty altogether—constituting so to speak a spoken alphabet. All speech in our language can be treated in practice as sequences of just those thirty elements, thus rectifying small deviations. Now outside the realm of language also there is probably only a rather limited alphabet of perceptual norms altogether, toward which we tend unconsciously to rectify all perceptions. These, if experimentally identified, could be taken as epistemological building blocks, the working elements of experience. They might prove in part to be culturally variable, as phonemes are, and in part universal.

Again there is the area that the psychologist Donald T. Campbell calls evolutionary epistemology.[9] In this area there is work by Hüseyin Yilmaz, who shows how some structural traits of color perception could have been predicted from survival value.[10] And a more emphatically epistemological topic that evolution helps to clarify is induction, now that we are allowing epistemology the resources of natural science.[11]

[9] D. T. Campbell, "Methodological suggestions from a comparative psychology of knowledge processes," *Inquiry* 2 (1959), 152–182.

[10] Hüseyin Yilmaz, "On color vision and a new approach to general perception," in E. E. Bernard and M. R. Kare, eds., *Biological Prototypes and Synthetic Systems* (New York: Plenum, 1962); "Perceptual invariance and the psychophysical law," *Perception and Psychophysics* 2 (1967), 533–538.

[11] See "Natural Kinds," Chapter 5 in this volume.

4

Existence
and
Quantification

The question whether there
are numbers, or qualities, or classes, is a metaphysical question, such as the logical positivists have regarded as meaningless. On the other hand the question whether there are rabbits,
or unicorns, is as meaningful as can be. A conspicuous difference is that bodies can be perceived. Still, this is not all that
matters; for we can evidently say also, meaningfully and without metaphysics, that there are prime numbers between 10 and
20.

What typifies the metaphysical cases is rather, according to
an early doctrine of Carnap's,[1] the use of category words, or
Allwörter. It is meaningful to ask whether there are prime
numbers between 10 and 20, but meaningless to ask in general
whether there are numbers; and likewise it is meaningful to
ask whether there are rabbits, or unicorns, but meaningless to
ask in general whether there are bodies.

But this ruling is unsatisfactory in two ways. The first difficulty is that there is no evident standard of what to count as a
category, or category word. Typically, in terms of formalized

[1] Carnap, *Logical Syntax of Language*, p. 292.

quantification theory, each category comprises the range of some distinctive style of variables. But the style of variable is an arbitrary matter, and surely of no help in distinguishing between meaningful questions of existence and metaphysical questions of existence. For there are no external constraints on styles of variables; we can use distinctive styles for different sorts of number, or a single style for all sorts of numbers and everything else as well. Notations with one style of variables and notations with many are intertranslatable.

There is another idea of category that may superficially seem more profound. It is the idea of semantic category, as Leśniewski called it,[2] or what linguists call a substitution class. Expressions belong to the same substitution class if, whenever you put one for the other in a meaningful sentence, you get a meaningful sentence. The question whether numbers constitute a category gives way, in these terms, to a question of the meaningfulness of the sentences that we obtain by supplanting number words by other words. However, what to count as meaningful is not at all clear. The empirical linguist manages the point after a fashion by considering what sentences could be elicited by reasonable means from naive native speakers. But such a criterion is of little value to a philosopher with a reform program. In fact, the question what existence sentences to count as meaningless was where we came in.

Existence questions were ruled meaningless by Carnap when they turned on category words. This was, I said, an unsatisfactory ruling in two respects. We have seen one of the respects: the tenuousness of the idea of category word. Now the other respect is that anyway sense needs to be made of categorial existence questions, however you choose your categories.

[2] Stanisław Leśniewski, "Grundzüge eines neuen Systems der Grundlagen der Mathematik," §§ 1–11, *Fundamenta Mathematicae* 14 (1929), pp. 1–81.

For it can happen in the austerest circles that some one will try to rework a mathematical system in such a way as to avoid assuming certain sorts of objects. He may try to get by with the assumption of just numbers and not sets of numbers; or he may try to get by with classes to the exclusion of properties; or he may try, like Whitehead, to avoid points and make do with extended regions and sets of regions. Clearly the system-maker in such cases is trying for something, and there is some distinction to be drawn between his getting it and not.

When we want to check on existence, bodies have it over other objects on the score of their perceptibility. But we have moved now to the question of checking not on existence, but on imputations of existence: on what a theory says exists. The question is when to maintain that a theory assumes a given object, or objects of a given sort—numbers, say, or sets of numbers, or properties, of points. To show that a theory assumes a given object, or objects of a given class, we have to show that the theory would be false if that object did not exist, or if that class were empty; hence that the theory requires that object, or members of that class, in order to be true. How are such requirements revealed?

Perhaps we find proper names of the objects. Still, this is no evidence that the objects are required, except as we can show that these proper names of the objects are used in the theory *as* proper names of the objects. The word "dog" may be used as a proper name of an animal species, but it may also be used merely as a general term true of each of various individuals and naming no one object at all; so the presence of the word is of itself no evidence that species are being assumed as objects. Again even "Pegasus," which is inflexibly a proper name grammatically speaking, can be used by persons who deny existence of its object. It is even used in denying that existence.

What would count then as evidence that an expression is

used in a theory as a name of an object? Let us represent the expression as "a." Now if the theory affirms the existentially quantified identity "$(\exists x)(x = a)$," certainly we have our answer: "a" is being used to name an object. In general we may say that an expression is used in a theory as naming if and only if the existentially quantified identity built on that expression is true according to the theory.

Of course we could also say, more simply, that "a" is used to name an object if and only if the statement "a exists" is true for the theory. This is less satisfactory only insofar as the meaning of "exists" may have seemed less settled than quantifiers and identity. We may indeed take "$(\exists x)(x = a)$" as explicating "a exists." John Bacon has noted a nice parallel here: [3] just as "a eats" is short for "a eats something," so "a is" is short for "a is something."

An expression "a" may occur in a theory, we saw, with or without purporting to name an object. What clinches matters is rather the quantification "$(\exists x)(x = a)$." It is the existential quantifier, not the "a" itself, that carries existential import. This is just what existential quantification is for, of course. It is a logically regimented rendering of the "there is" idiom. The bound variable "x" ranges over the universe, and the existential quantification says that at least one of the objects in the universe satisfies the appended condition—in this case the condition of being the object a. To show that some given object is required in a theory, what we have to show is no more nor less than that that object is required, for the truth of the theory, to be among the values over which the bound variables range.

Appreciation of this point affords us more than an explication of "a exists," since the existentially quantified identity "$(\exists x)(x = a)$" is one case of existential quantification among

[3] J. Bacon, *Being and Existence*, dissertation, Yale, 1966.

many. It is a case where the value of the variable that is said to exist is an object with a name; the name is "*a*." This is the way with singular existence sentences generally, sentences of the form "*a* exists" or "There is such a thing as *a*," but it is not the way with existence sentences generally. For instance, under classical set theory there are, given any interpreted notation, some real numbers that are not separately specifiable in that notation. The existence sentence "There are unspecifiable real numbers" is true, and expressible as an existential quantification; but the values of the variable that account for the truth of this quantification are emphatically not objects with names. Here then is another reason why quantified variables, not names, are what to look to for the existential force of a theory.

Another way of saying what objects a theory requires is to say that they are the objects that some of the predicates of the theory have to be true of, in order for the theory to be true. But this is the same as saying that they are the objects that have to be values of the variables in order for the theory to be true. It is the same, anyway, if the notation of the theory includes for each predicate a complementary predicate, its negation. For then, given any value of a variable, some predicate is true of it; viz., any predicate or its complement. And conversely, of course, whatever a predicate is true of is a value of variables. Predication and quantification, indeed, are intimately linked; for a predicate is simply any expression that yields a sentence, an open sentence, when adjoined to one or more quantifiable variables. When we schematize a sentence in the predicative way "*Fa*," or "*a* is an *F*," our recognition of an "*a*" part and an "*F*" part turns strictly on our use of variables of quantification; the "*a*" represents a part of the sentence that stands where a quantifiable variable could stand, and the "*F*" represents the rest.

Our question was: what objects does a theory require? Our answer is: those objects that have to be values of variables for the theory to be true. Of course a theory may, in this sense, require no objects in particular, and still not tolerate an empty universe of discourse either, for the theory might be fulfilled equally by either of two mutually exclusive universes. If for example the theory implies "$(\exists x)(x$ is a dog$)$," it will not tolerate an empty universe; still the theory might be fulfilled by a universe that contained collies to the exclusion of spaniels, and also vice versa. So there is more to be said of a theory, ontologically, than just saying what objects, if any, the theory requires; we can also ask what various universes would be severally sufficient. The specific objects required, if any, are the objects common to all those universes.

I think mainly of single-sorted quantification; i.e., a single style of variables. As remarked, the many-sorted is translatable into one-sorted. Generally such translation has the side effect of admitting as meaningful some erstwhile meaningless predications. E.g., if the predicate "divisible by 3" is henceforth to be trained on general variables instead of number variables, we must make sense of calling things other than numbers divisible by 3. But this is easy; we may count such attributions false instead of meaningless. In general, thus, the reduction of many-sorted quantification to one-sorted has the effect of merging some substitution classes; more words become meaningfully interchangeable.

Carnap's reservations over *Allwörter* now cease to apply, and so his special strictures against philosophical questions of existence lapse as well. To what extent have we meanwhile become clearer on such questions of existence? On the higher-order question, what things a theory assumes there to be, we have gained a pointer: look to the behavior of quantified variables and don't cavil about names. Regarding the meaning of existence itself our progress is less clear.

Existence is what existential quantification expresses. There are things of kind F if and only if $(\exists x)Fx$. This is as unhelpful as it is undebatable, since it is how one explains the symbolic notation of quantification to begin with. The fact is that it is unreasonable to ask for an explication of existence in simpler terms. We found an explication of singular existence, "a exists," as "$(\exists x)(x = a)$"; but explication in turn of the existential quantifier itself, "there is," "there are," explication of general existence, is a forlorn cause. Further understanding we may still seek even here, but not in the form of explication. We may still ask what counts as evidence for existential quantifications.

To this question there is no simple, general answer. If the open sentence under the quantifier is something like "x is a rabbit" or "x is a unicorn," then the evidence, if any, is largely the testimony of the senses. If the open sentence is "x is a prime number between 10 and 20," the evidence lies in computation. If the open sentence is merely "x is a number," or "x is a class," or the like, the evidence is much harder to pinpoint. But I think the positivists were mistaken when they despaired of evidence in such cases and accordingly tried to draw up boundaries that would exclude such sentences as meaningless. Existence statements in this philosophical vein do admit of evidence, in the sense that we can have reasons, and essentially scientific reasons, for including numbers or classes or the like in the range of values of our variables. And other existence statements in this metaphysical vein can be subject to counter-evidence; we can have essentially scientific reasons for excluding propositions, perhaps, or attributes, or unactualized bodies, from the range of our variables. Numbers and classes are favoured by the power and facility which they contribute to theoretical physics and other systematic discourse about nature. Propositions and attributes are disfavored by some irregular behaviour in connection with identity and substitution. Considerations for and against existence are more broadly systematic, in these philosophical examples, than in the case of rabbits or unicorns or prime numbers between 10 and 20; but I am persuaded that the difference is a matter of degree. Our theory of nature grades off from the most concrete fact to speculations about the curvature of space-time, or the continuous creation of hydrogen atoms in an expanding universe; and our evidence grades off correspondingly, from specific observation to broadly systematic considerations. Existential quantifications of the philosophical sort belong to the same inclusive theory and are situated way out at the end, farthest from observable fact.

Thus far I have been playing down the difference between commonsense existence statements, as of rabbits and unicorns, and philosophical existence statements, as of numbers and attributes. But there is also a curious difference between commonsense existence statements and philosophical ones that needs to be played up, and it is one that can be appreciated already right in among the rabbits. For let us reflect that a theory might accommodate all rabbit data and yet admit as values of its variables no rabbits or other bodies but only qualities, times, and places. The adherents of that theory, or *immaterialists*, would have a sentence which, as a whole, had the same stimulus meaning as our sentence "There is a rabbit in the yard"; yet in the quantificational sense of the words they would have to deny that there is a rabbit in the yard or anywhere else. Here, then, prima facie, are two senses of existence of rabbits, a common sense and a philosophical sense.

A similar distinction can be drawn in the case of the prime

numbers between 10 and 20. Suppose someone has for reasons of nominalism renounced most of mathematics and settled for bodies as sole values of his variables. He can still do such part of arithmetic as requires no variables. In particular he can still subscribe to the nine-clause alternation "11 is prime or 12 is prime or 13 is prime or . . . or 19 is prime." In this sense he agrees with us that there are primes between 10 and 20, but in the quantificational sense he denies that there are primes or numbers at all.

Shall we say: so much the worse for a quantificational version of existence? Hardly; we already found this version trivial but undebatable. Are there then two senses of existence? Only in a derivative way. For us common men who believe in bodies and prime numbers, the statements "There is a rabbit in the yard" and "There are prime numbers between 10 and 20" are free from double-talk. Quantification does them justice. When we come to the immaterialist, and we tell him there is a rabbit in the yard, he will know better than to demur on account of his theory; he will acquiesce on account of a known holophrastic relation of stimulus synonymy between our sentence and some sentence geared to his different universe. In practice he will even stoop to our idiom himself, both to facilitate communication and because of speech habits lingering from his own benighted youth. This he will do when the theoretical question is not at issue, just as we speak of the sun as rising. Insofar we may say, I grant, that there are for him two senses of existence; but there is no confusion, and the theoretical use is rather to be respected as literal and basic than deplored as a philosophical disorder.

Similar remarks apply to our nominalist. He will agree that there are primes between 10 and 20, when we are talking arithmetic and not philosophy. When we turn to philosophy he will condone that usage as a mere manner of speaking, and offer the paraphrase. Similar remarks apply to us; many of our casual remarks in the "there are" form would want dusting up when our thoughts turn seriously ontological. Each time, if a point is made of it, the burden is of course on us to paraphrase or retract.

It has been fairly common in philosophy early and late to distinguish between being, as the broadest concept, and existence, as narrower. This is no distinction of mine; I mean "exists" to cover all there is, and such of course is the force of the quantifier. For those who do make the distinction, the existent tends to be on the concrete or temporal side. Now there was perhaps a reminder of the distinction in the case of the rabbit and the immaterialist. At that point two senses of "there is," a common and a philosophical, threatened to diverge. Perhaps the divergence which that sort of case suggests has been one factor in making philosophers receptive to a distinction between existence and being. Anyway, it ought not to. For the point there was that the rabbit was not a value of the immaterialist's variables; thus existence, if this were the analogy, would not be a species of being. Moreover, we saw that the sensible materiality of the rabbit was inessential to the example, since the prime numbers between 10 and 20 sustained much the same point.

Along with the annoying practice of restricting the term "existence" to a mere species of what there is, there is Meinong's bizarre deviation of an opposite kind. *Gegenstände* or objects, for him, comprised more even than what there was; an object might or might not be. His notion of object was, as Chisholm puts it, *jenseits von Sein und Nichtsein.*[4] Oddly enough I find

4 Roderick M. Chisholm, "Jenseits von Sein und Nichtsein," K. S. Guthke, ed., *Dichtung und Deutung* (Bern and Munich: Francke, 1961).

this idea a good one, provided that we bolster it with Bentham's theory of fictions. Contextual definition, or what Bentham called paraphrasis, can enable us to talk very considerably and conveniently about putative objects without footing an ontological bill. It is a strictly legitimate way of making theories in which there is less than meets the eye.

Bentham's idea of paraphrasis flowered late, in Russell's theory of descriptions. Russell's theory affords a rigorous and important example of how expressions can be made to parade as names and then be explained away as a mere manner of speaking, by explicit paraphrase of the context into an innocent notation. However, Russell's theory of descriptions was less a way of simulating objects than of contextually defining terms to designate real objects. When the description fails to specify anything, Russell accommodates it grudgingly: he makes its immediate sentential contexts uniformly false.

Where we find Russell exploiting paraphrasis for simulation of objects is not in his theory of descriptions but rather in his contextual theory of classes. There are really no such things as classes, according to him, but he simulates discourse about classes by contextual definition, and not grudgingly; not just by making all immediate contexts false.

There is a well-known catch to Russell's theory of classes. The theory depends on an unheralded but irreducible assumption of attributes as values of bound variables. Russell only reduces classes to attributes, and this can scarcely be viewed as a reduction in the right direction unless for wrong reasons.

But it is possible by paraphrasis to introduce a certain amount of class talk, less than Russell's, without really assuming attributes or any other objects beyond the ones wanted as members of the simulated classes. I developed this line somewhat under the head of virtual classes, long ago, and Richard

Martin was at it independently at that time.[5] Lately I made much use of it in *Set Theory and Its Logic*. What it yields is substantial enough to implant new hopes, in many breasts, of making do with a nominalist ontology. Unfortunately these would have to be breasts unmindful of the needs of mathematics. For of itself the virtual theory of classes affords no adequate foundation for the classical mathematics even of the positive integers. However, it is handy still as a supplementary technique after we have bowed to the need of assuming real classes too; for it enables us to simulate further classes beyond those assumed. For that reason, and also because I think it good strategy in all subjects to postpone assumptions until needed, I am in favor of exploiting the virtual theory for all it is worth.

Virtual classes do not figure as values of bound variables. They owe their utility partly to a conventional use of schematic letters, which, though not quantifiable, behave like free variables. The simulated names of the virtual classes are substitutable for such letters. We could even call these letters free variables, if we resist the temptation to bind them. Virtual classes can then be seen as simulated values of these simulated variables. Hintikka has presented a logic, not specifically of classes but of entities and non-entities generally, in which the non-entities figure thus as values only of free variables.[6] Or, to speak less figuratively, the singular terms which fail to designate can be substituted only for free variables, whereas singu-

[5] R. M. Martin, "A homogeneous system of formal logic," *Journal of Symbolic Logic* 8 (1943), 1–23.

[6] Jaakko Hintikka, "Existential presuppositions and existential commitments," *Journal of Philosophy* 56 (1959), 125–137. For a bigger venture in this direction see Henry S. Leonard, "Essences, attributes, and predicates," *Proceedings and Addresses of the American Philosophical Association* 37 (1964), 25–51.

lar terms which do designate can be used also in instantiating quantification.

So much for simulated objects. I want now to go back and pick up a loose end where we were considering the immaterialist. I said he would fall in with our statement "There is a rabbit in the yard" just to convey agreement on the stimulus content, or even out of habit carried over from youth. But what about the alternative situation where the immaterialist is not a deviant Western intellectual, but a speaker of an unknown language which we are bent on construing? Suddenly the conditions themselves become problematical. In principle there is no difficulty in equating a sentence of his holophrastically, by stimulus meaning, with our sentence "There is a rabbit in the yard." But how could it ever be determined, even in probabilistic terms, that his ontology includes qualities, times, and places, and excludes bodies? I argued in *Word and Object* that such ontological questions regarding a radically alien language make no objective sense. In principle we could devise any of various sets of analytical hypotheses for translating the language into ours; many such sets can conform fully to all evidence and even be behaviorally equivalent to one another, and yet disagree with one another as to the native's equivalents of our predicates and quantifiers. For practical translation we fix on one of the adequate sets of analytical hypotheses, and in the light of it we report even on the native's ontology; but what to report is uniquely determined neither by evidence nor by fact. There is no fact of the matter.

Consider, in contrast, the truth functions. We can state substantial behavioral conditions for interpreting a native sentence connective as, say, alternation. The requirement is that the natives be disposed to dissent from any compound statement, formed by the connective in question, when and only when disposed to dissent from each of the component statements, and that they be disposed to assent to the compound whenever disposed to assent to a component. These conditions remain indeed less than definitive on one point: on the question of a native's assenting to the compound but to neither component. For instance we may affirm of two horses that one or the other will win, and still not be prepared to affirm of either one that he will win.[7] Still, the two conditions do much toward identifying alternation; more than any behavioral conditions can do for quantification. And it is easy to do as well for the other truth functions as for alternation.

There is indeed a variant of quantification, favored by Leśniewski and by Ruth Marcus,[8] which does admit behavioural criteria of translation as substantial as those for the truth functions. I shall call it *substitutional* quantification. An existential substitutional quantification is counted as true if and only if there is an expression which, when substituted for the variable, makes the open sentence after the quantifier come out true. A universal quantification is counted as true if no substitution makes the open sentence come out false. Behavioral conditions for interpreting a native construction as existential substitutional quantification, then, are readily formulated. We fix on parts of the construction as candidates for the roles of quantifier and variable; then a condition of their fitness is that the natives be disposed to dissent from a whole quantified sentence when and only when disposed to dissent from each of the sentences obtainable by dropping the quantifier and substituting for the variable. A second condition is that the natives

---

[7] In *Word and Object*, p. 58, I gave only the condition on dissent and so overlooked this limitation on the assent side. Conjunction suffered in equal and opposite fashion.

[8] See above, p. 63n.

be disposed to assent to the whole whenever disposed to assent to one of the sentences obtainable by dropping the quantifier and substituting for the variable. As in the case of alternation, the behavioural conditions do not wholly settle assent; but they go far. Analogous criteria for universal substitutional quantification are equally evident.

Naturally we never expect mathematical certainty as to whether such a behavioral criterion is fulfilled by a given construction in the native language. For any one choice of native locutions as candidates for the role of quantifier and variable, an infinite lot of quantified sentences and substitution instances would have to be tested. The behavioral criteria for the truth functions are similar in this respect. Empirical induction is all we have to go on, and all we would ask.

Substitutional quantification and the truth functions are, in brief, far and away more recognizable behaviorally than classical quantification, or what we may call *objectual* quantification. We can locate objectual quantification in our own language because we grow up using those very words: if not the actual quantifiers, then words like "exists" and "there is" by which they come to be explained to us. We can locate it in other languages only relative to chosen or inherited codes of translation which are in a sense arbitrary. They are arbitrary in the sense that they could be materially different and still conform to all the same behavior apart from the behavior of translation itself. Objectual quantification is in this sense more parochial than substitutional quantification and the truth functions.

In his substitutional quantification Leśniewski used different styles of variables for different substitution classes. Substitutional quantification in the substitution class of singular terms, or names, is the sort that comes closest to objectual quantification. But it is clearly not equivalent to it—not unless each of our objects is specifiable by some singular term or other in our language, and no term of that substitution class fails to specify an object. For this reason substitutional quantification gives no acceptable version of existence properly so-called, not if objectual quantification does. Moreover, substitutional quantification makes good sense, explicable in terms of truth and substitution, no matter what substitution class we take—even that whose sole member is the left-hand parenthesis.[9] To conclude that entities are being assumed that trivially, and that far out, is simply to drop ontological questions. Nor can we introduce any control by saying that only substitutional quantification in the substitution class of singular terms is to count as a version of existence. We just now saw one reason for this, and there is another: the very notion of singular terms appeals implicitly to classical or objectual quantification. This is the point that I made earlier about analyzing sentences according to the scheme "*Fa.*" Leśniewski did not himself relate his kind of quantification to ontological commitments.

This does not mean that theories using substitutional quantification and no objectual quantification can get on *without* objects. I hold rather that the question of the ontological commitment of a theory does not properly arise except as that theory is expressed in classical quantificational form, or insofar as one has in mind how to translate it into that form. I hold this for the simple reason that the existential quantifier, in the objectual sense, is given precisely the existential interpretation and no other: there are things which are thus and so.

It is easy to see how substitutional quantification might be translated into a theory of standard form. Consider a substitutional quantification whose quantifier is existential and contains the variable v and governs the open sentence S. We can paraphrase it in syntactical and semantical terms, with objectual quantification, thus: there is an expression which, put for v in S, yields a truth. Universal quantification can be handled similarly. For this method the theory into which we translate is one that talks about expressions of the original theory, and assumes them among its objects—as values of its variables of objectual quantification. By arithmetized syntax, natural numbers would do as well. Thus we may look upon substitutional quantification not as avoiding all ontological commitment, but as getting by with, in effect, a universe of natural numbers.

Substitutional quantification has its points. If I could see my way to getting by with an all-purpose universe whose objects were denumerable and indeed enumerated, I would name each object numerically and settle for substitutional quantification. I would consider this an advance epistemologically, since substitutional quantification is behaviorally better determined than objectual quantification. Here then is a new reason, if one were needed, for aspiring to a denumerable universe.

In switching at that point to substitutional quantification we would not, as already stressed, reduce our denumerable universe to a null universe. We would, however, turn our backs on ontological questions. Where substitutional quantification serves, ontology lacks point. The ontology of such a theory is worth trying to elicit only when we are making translations or other comparisons between that theory and a theory which, because of an indenumerable or indefinite universe, is irreducibly committed to something like objectual quantification. Indenumerable and indefinite universes are what, in the end, give point to objectual quantification and ontology.[10]

[10] The foregoing reflections on substitutional quantification were elicited largely by discussions with Burton Dreben. On the pointlessness of ontology at the denumerable level see also my *Ways of Paradox*, p. 203.

I urged that objectual quantification, more than substitutional quantification, is in a sense parochial. Then so is the idea of being; for objectual existential quantification was devised outright for "there is." But still one may ask, and Hao Wang has asked, whether we do not represent being in an unduly parochial way when we equate it strictly with our own particular quantification theory to the exclusion of somewhat deviant quantification theories. Substitutional quantification indeed would not serve as an account of being, for reasons already noted; but what of intuitionistic quantification theory, or other deviations? [11] Now one answer is that it would indeed be a reasonable use of words to say that the intuitionist has a different doctrine of being from mine, as he has a different quantification theory; and that I am simply at odds with the intuitionist on the one as on the other. When I try to determine the universe of someone else's theory, I use "being" my way. In particular thus I might come out with a different inventory of an intuitionist's universe than the intuitionist, with his deviant sense of being, would come out with. Or I might simply see no satisfactory translation of his notation into mine, and so conclude that the question of his ontology cannot be raised in terms acceptable to me.

But this answer misses an important element in Wang's question. Namely, how much better than arbitrary is our particular quantification theory, seen as one in some possible spectrum of quantification theories? Misgivings in this direction can be fostered by noting the following form of sentence, due essentially to Henkin: [12]

[11] One such, propounded by Leonard, "Essences, attributes, and predicates," p. 39, combines substitutional and objectual quantification.

[12] Leon Henkin, "Some remarks on infinitely long formulas," *Infinitistic Methods* (proceedings of a Warsaw symposium) (New York: Pergamon, 1961), pp. 167–183, specifically p. 181.

(1) Each thing bears P to something y and each thing bears Q to something w such that Ryw.

The best we can do for this in ordinary quantificational terms is:

(2) $\qquad (x)(\exists y)(Pxy \,.\, (z)(\exists w)(Qzw \,.\, Ryw)\,)$

or equally:

(3) $\qquad (z)(\exists w)(Qzw \,.\, (x)(\exists y)(Pxy \,.\, Ryw)\,).$

These are not equivalent. (2) represents the choice of y as independent of z; (3) does not. (3) represents the choice of w as independent of x; (2) does not. Moreover there are interpretations of P, Q, and R in (1) that make both dependences gratuitous; for instance, interpretation of P as "is part of," Q as "contains," and R as "is bigger than."

(4) Each thing is part of something y and each thing contains something w such that y is bigger than w.

One may suspect that the notation of quantification is at fault in forcing a choice between (2) and (3) in a case like this.

By admitting functions as values of our bound variables, Henkin observes, we can escape the limitations of (2) and (3) as follows:

(5) $\qquad (\exists f)(\exists g)(x)(z)(Pxf_x \,.\, Qzg_z \,.\, Rf_x g_z).$

But this move assumes higher-order objects, which may seem out of keeping with the elementary character of (1). Henkin then points out a liberalization of the classical quantification notation which does the work of (5) without quantifying over functions. Just allow branching quantifiers, thus:

$$\begin{matrix} (x)(\exists y) & \\ & (Pxy \,.\, Qzw \,.\, Ryw). \\ (z)(\exists w) & \end{matrix}$$

(6)

One may feel, therefore, that an ontological standard geared to classical quantification theory is overcritical. It would interpret (4) as assuming functions, by interpreting it as (5), whereas the deviant quantification theory with its branching quantifiers would interpret (4) more plausibly as not talking of any functions. And it would do so without slipping into the inappropriate bias of (2), or that of (3).

One is tempted further by the following considerations. The second-order formula (5) is of a kind that I shall call *functionally existential,* meaning that all its function quantifiers are out in front and existential. Now there is a well-known complete proof procedure of Skolem's for classical quantification theory, which consists in showing a formula inconsistent by taking what I call its functional normal form and deriving a truth-functional contradiction from it.[13] Anyone familiar with the procedure can quickly see that it works not only for all first-order formulas, that is, all formulas in the notation of classical quantification theory, but all these functionally existential formulas as well. Any inconsistent formula not only of classical quantification theory, but of this functionally existential annex, can be shown inconsistent by one and the same method of functional normal forms. This makes the annex seem pretty integral. One is tempted to seek further notational departures, in the first-orderish spirit of the branching quantifiers, which would suffice to accommodate all the functionally existential formulas the way (6) accommodates (5). Henkin has in fact devised a general notation of this kind.

By considerations of duality, moreover, these reflections upon functionally existential formulas can be paralleled with regard to functionally universal formulas—those whose function quantifiers are out in front and universal. Skolem's method of proving inconsistency has as its dual a method of proving validity, and it works not only for all first-order formulas but for all these functionally universal formulas as well. Thus this

[13] See my *Selected Logic Papers,* pp. 196 ff.

still further annex would be every bit as integral as the functionally existential one. We seem to see our way, then, to so enlarging classical quantification theory as to gain all the extra power that would have been afforded by assuming functions, so long as the function quantifiers were out in front and all existential or all universal. It would mean a grateful slackening of our ontological accountability.

These reflections encourage the idea that our classical logic of quantification is arbitrarily restrictive. However, I shall now explain what I think to be a still weightier counter-consideration. The classical logic of quantification has a complete proof procedure for validity and a complete proof procedure for inconsistency; indeed each procedure serves both purposes, since a formula is valid if and only if its negation is inconsistent. The most we can say for the functionally existential annex, on the other hand, is that it has a complete proof procedure for inconsistency; and the most we can say for the functionally universal annex is that it has a complete proof procedure for validity. The trick of proving a formula valid by proving its negation inconsistent, or vice versa, is not applicable in the annexes, since in general the negation of a functionally existential formula is not equivalent to a functionally existential formula (but only to a functionally universal one), and conversely. In fact there is a theorem due to Craig [14] which shows that the negation of a functionally existential formula is never equivalent to a functionally existential formula, unless the functions were superfluous and the formula was equivalent to a first-order formula; and correspondingly for functionally universal formulas. Thus classical, unsupplemented quantification theory is on this score maximal: it is as far out as you can go and still

[14] William Craig, "Three uses of the Herbrand-Gentzen theorem," *Journal of Symbolic Logic* 22 (1957), 269–285, specifically 281.

have complete coverage of validity and inconsistency by the Skolem proof procedure.

Henkin even shows that the valid formulas which are quantified merely in the fourfold fashion shown in (5), or (6), are already more than can be covered by any proof procedure, at any rate when identity is included.[15]

Here then is a reason to draw boundaries in such a way as to regard (6) as talking covertly of functions after all, and as receiving a just analysis in (5). On this view (1) is not the proper business of pure quantification theory after all, but treats of functions. That is, if the form (1) is not to be read with the bias (2) or the bias (3), it is to be explained as (5).

We may be somewhat reconciled to this conclusion by an observation of Jean van Heijenoort, to the effect that (1) is not after all very ordinary language; its grammar is doubtful. Can the "such that" reach back across the "and" to cover the "y"? If assignment of meaning to extraordinary language is what we are about, we may indeed assign (5) and not wonder at its being irreducibly of second order.

Since introducing (1), I have proved nothing. I have explained two sorts of considerations, one to illustrate how we might be led to see the classical state of quantification theory as arbitrary, and the other to illustrate how it is better than arbitrary. Classical quantification theory enjoys an extraordi-

[15] Henkin, "Some remarks on infinitely long formulas," p. 182 and footnote. Henkin derives this conclusion from a theorem of Mostowski by an argument which he credits to Ehrenfeucht.

I am indebted to Peter Geach for first bringing the question of (1) to my attention, in January 1960; and I am indebted to my colleagues Burton Dreben and Saul Kripke and my pupil Christopher Hill for steering me to pertinent papers. Dreben's advice has been helpful also elsewhere.

nary combination of depth and simplicity, beauty and utility. It is bright within and bold in its boundaries. Deviations from it are likely, in contrast, to look rather arbitrary. But insofar as they exist it seems clearest and simplest to say that deviant concepts of existence exist along with them.

5

Natural
Kinds

What tends to confirm an induction? This question has been aggravated on the one hand by Hempel's puzzle of the non-black non-ravens,[1] and exacerbated on the other by Goodman's puzzle of the grue emeralds.[2] I shall begin my remarks by relating the one puzzle to the other, and the other to an innate flair that we have for natural kinds. Then I shall devote the rest of the paper to reflections on the nature of this notion of natural kinds and its relation to science.

Hempel's puzzle is that just as each black raven tends to confirm the law that all ravens are black, so each green leaf, being a non-black non-raven, should tend to confirm the law that all non-black things are non-ravens, that is, again, that all ravens are black. What is paradoxical is that a green leaf should count toward the law that all ravens are black.

[1] C. G. Hempel, *Aspects of Scientific Explanation and Other Essays* (New York: Free Press, 1965), p. 15.

[2] Nelson Goodman, *Fact, Fiction, and Forecast* (Cambridge, Mass., 1955, or New York: Bobbs-Merrill, 1965), p. 74. I am indebted to Goodman and to Burton Dreben for helpful criticisms of earlier drafts of the present paper.

Goodman propounds his puzzle by requiring us to imagine that emeralds, having been identified by some criterion other than color, are now being examined one after another and all up to now are found to be green. Then he proposes to call anything *grue* that is examined today or earlier and found to be green or is not examined before tomorrow and is blue. Should we expect the first one examined tomorrow to be green, because all examined up to now were green? But all examined up to now were also grue; so why not expect the first one tomorrow to be grue, and therefore blue?

The predicate "green," Goodman says,[3] is *projectible;* "grue" is not. He says this by way of putting a name to the problem. His step toward solution is his doctrine of what he calls entrenchment,[4] which I shall touch on later. Meanwhile the terminological point is simply that projectible predicates are predicates ζ and η whose shared instances all do count, for whatever reason, toward confirmation of $\ulcorner$All ζ are $\eta\urcorner$.

Now I propose assimilating Hempel's puzzle to Goodman's by inferring from Hempel's that the complement of a projectible predicate need not be projectible. "Raven" and "black" are projectible; a black raven does count toward "All ravens are black." Hence a black raven counts also, indirectly, toward "No non-black things are non-ravens," since this says the same thing. But a green leaf does not count toward "All non-black things are non-ravens," nor, therefore, toward "All ravens are black"; "non-black" and "non-raven" are not projectible. "Green" and "leaf" are projectible, and the green leaf counts toward "All leaves are green" and "All green things are leaves"; but only a black raven can confirm "All ravens are black," the complements not being projectible.

---

[3] Goodman, *Fact*, pp. 82 f.
[4] *Ibid.*, pp. 95 ff.

If we see the matter in this way, we must guard against saying that a statement ⌜All ζ are η⌝ is lawlike only if ζ and η are projectible. "All non-black things are non-ravens" is a law despite its non-projectible terms, since it is equivalent to "All ravens are black." Any statement is lawlike that is logically *equivalent* to ⌜All ζ are η⌝ for some projectible ζ and η.[5]

Having concluded that the complement of a projectible predicate need not be projectible, we may ask further whether there is *any* projectible predicate whose complement is projectible. I can conceive that there is not, when complements are taken strictly. We must not be misled by limited or relative complementation; "male human" and "non-male human" are indeed both projectible.

To get back now to the emeralds, why do we expect the next one to be green rather than grue? The intuitive answer lies in similarity, however subjective. Two green emeralds are more similar than two grue ones would be if only one of the grue ones were green. Green things, or at least green emeralds, are a kind.[6] A projectible predicate is one that is true of all and only the things of a kind. What makes Goodman's example a puzzle, however, is the dubious scientific standing of a general notion of similarity, or of kind.

The dubiousness of this notion is itself a remarkable fact. For surely there is nothing more basic to thought and language than our sense of similarity; our sorting of things into kinds. The usual general term, whether a common noun or a verb or an adjective, owes its generality to some resemblance among the things referred to. Indeed, learning to use a word de-

[5] I mean this only as a sufficient condition of lawlikeness. See Donald Davidson, "Emeroses by other names," *Journal of Philosophy* 63 (1966), 778-780.

[6] This relevance of kind is noted by Goodman, *Fact*, first edition, pp. 119 f; second edition, pp. 121 f.

pends on a double resemblance: first, a resemblance between the present circumstances and past circumstances in which the word was used, and second, a phonetic resemblance between the present utterance of the word and past utterances of it. And every reasonable expectation depends on resemblance of circumstances, together with our tendency to expect similar causes to have similar effects.

The notion of a kind and the notion of similarity or resemblance seem to be variants or adaptations of a single notion. Similarity is immediately definable in terms of kind; for, things are similar when they are two of a kind. The very words for "kind" and "similar" tend to run in etymologically cognate pairs. Cognate with "kind" we have "akin" and "kindred." Cognate with "like" we have "ilk." Cognate with "similar" and "same" and "resemble" there are "*sammeln*" and "assemble," suggesting a gathering into kinds.

We cannot easily imagine a more familiar or fundamental notion than this, or a notion more ubiquitous in its applications. On this score it is like the notions of logic: like identity, negation, alternation, and the rest. And yet, strangely, there is something logically repugnant about it. For we are baffled when we try to relate the general notion of similarity significantly to logical terms. One's first hasty suggestion might be to say that things are similar when they have all or most or many properties in common. Or, trying to be less vague, one might try defining comparative similarity—"a is more similar to b than to c"—as meaning that a shares more properties with b than with c. But any such course only reduces our problem to the unpromising task of settling what to count as a property.

The nature of the problem of what to count as a property can be seen by turning for a moment to set theory. Things are viewed as going together into sets in any and every combination, describable and indescribable. Any two things are joint members of any number of sets. Certainly then we cannot define "*a* is more similar to *b* than to *c*" to mean that *a* and *b* belong jointly to more sets than *a* and *c* do. If properties are to support this line of definition where sets do not, it must be because properties do not, like sets, take things in every random combination. It must be that properties are shared only by things that are significantly similar. But properties in such a sense are no clearer than kinds. To start with such a notion of property, and define similarity on that basis, is no better than accepting similarity as undefined.

The contrast between properties and sets which I suggested just now must not be confused with the more basic and familiar contrast between properties, as intensional, and sets as extensional. Properties are intensional in that they may be counted as distinct properties even though wholly coinciding in respect of the things that have them. There is no call to reckon kinds as intensional. Kinds can be seen as sets, determined by their members. It is just that not all sets are kinds.

If similarity is taken simple-mindedly as a yes-or-no affair, with no degrees, then there is no containing of kinds within broader kinds. For, as remarked, similarity now simply means belonging to some one same kind. If all colored things comprise a kind, then all colored things count as similar, and the set of all red things is too narrow to count as a kind. If on the other hand the set of all red things counts as a kind, then colored things do not all count as similar, and the set of all colored things is too broad to count as a kind. We cannot have it both ways. Kinds can, however, overlap; the red things can comprise one kind, the round another.

When we move up from the simple dyadic relation of similarity to the more serious and useful triadic relation of comparative similarity, a correlative change takes place in the notion of kind. Kinds come to admit now not only of overlapping but also of containment one in another. The set of all red things and the set of all colored things can now both count as kinds; for all colored things can now be counted as resembling one another more than some things do, even though less, on the whole, than red ones do.

At this point, of course, our trivial definition of similarity as sameness of kind breaks down; for almost any two things could count now as common members of some broad kind or other, and anyway we now want to define comparative or triadic similarity. A definition that suggests itself is this: a is more similar to b than to c when a and b belong jointly to more kinds than a and c do. But even this works only for finite systems of kinds.

The notion of kind and the notion of similarity seemed to be substantially one notion. We observed further that they resist reduction to less dubious notions, as of logic or set theory. That they at any rate be definable each in terms of the other seems little enough to ask. We just saw a somewhat limping definition of comparative similarity in terms of kinds. What now of the converse project, definition of kind in terms of similarity?

One may be tempted to picture a kind, suitable to a comparative similarity relation, as any set which is "qualitatively spherical" in this sense: it takes in exactly the things that differ less than so-and-so much from some central norm. If without serious loss of accuracy we can assume that there are one or more actual things (*paradigm cases*) that nicely exemplify the desired norm, and one or more actual things (*foils*) that deviate just barely too much to be counted into the desired kind at all, then our definition is easy: *the kind with paradigm a and foil b is the set of all the things to which a is more similar* than a is to b. More generally, then, a set may be said to be a *kind* if and only if there are a and b, known or unknown, such that the set is the kind with paradigm a and foil b.

If we consider examples, however, we see that this definition does not give us what we want as kinds. Thus take red. Let us grant that a central shade of red can be picked as norm. The trouble is that the paradigm cases, objects in just that shade of red, can come in all sorts of shapes, weights, sizes, and smells. Mere degree of overall similarity to any one such paradigm case will afford little evidence of degree of redness, since it will depend also on shape, weight, and the rest. If our assumed relation of comparative similarity were just comparative chromatic similarity, then our paradigm-and-foil definition of kind would indeed accommodate redkind. What the definition will not do is distill purely chromatic kinds from mixed similarity.

A different attempt, adapted from Carnap, is this: a set is a kind if all its members are more similar to one another than they all are to any one thing outside the set. In other words, each non-member differs more from some member than that member differs from any member. However, as Goodman showed in a criticism of Carnap,[7] this construction succumbs to what Goodman calls the difficulty of imperfect community. Thus consider the set of all red round things, red wooden things, and round wooden things. Each member of this set resembles each other member somehow: at least in being red, or in being round, or in being wooden, and perhaps in two or all three of these respects or others. Conceivably, moreover, there is no one thing outside the set that resembles every member of the set to even the least of these degrees. The set then meets the proposed definition of kind. Yet surely it is not what any-

[7] Nelson Goodman, *The Structure of Appearance*, 2d ed. (New York: Bobbs-Merrill, 1966), pp. 163 f.

one means by a kind. It admits yellow croquet balls and red rubber balls while excluding yellow rubber balls.

The relation between similarity and kind, then, is less clear and neat than could be wished. Definition of similarity in terms of kind is halting, and definition of kind in terms of similarity is unknown. Still the two notions are in an important sense correlative. They vary together. If we reassess something *a* as less similar to *b* than to *c*, where it had counted as more similar to *b* than to *c*, surely we will correspondingly permute *a*, *b*, and *c* in respect of their assignment to kinds; and conversely.

I have stressed how fundamental the notion of similarity or of kind is to our thinking, and how alien to logic and set theory. I want to go on now to say more about how fundamental these notions are to our thinking, and something also about their non-logical roots. Afterward I want to bring out how the notion of similarity or of kind changes as science progresses. I shall suggest that it is a mark of maturity of a branch of science that the notion of similarity or kind finally dissolves, so far as it is relevant to that branch of science. That is, it ultimately submits to analysis in the special terms of that branch of science and logic.

For deeper appreciation of how fundamental similarity is, let us observe more closely how it figures in the learning of language. One learns by *ostension* what presentations to call yellow; that is, one learns by hearing the word applied to samples. All he has to go on, of course, is the similarity of further cases to the samples. Similarity being a matter of degree, one has to learn by trial and error how reddish or brownish or greenish a thing can be and still be counted yellow. When he finds he has applied the word too far out, he can use the false cases as samples to the contrary; and then he can proceed to guess whether further cases are yellow or not by considering whether they are more similar to the in-group or the out-group. What one thus uses, even at this primitive stage of learning, is a fully functioning sense of similarity, and relative similarity at that: a is more similar to b than to c.

All these delicate comparisons and shrewd inferences about what to call yellow are, in Sherlock Holmes's terminology, elementary. Mostly the process is unconscious. It is the same process by which an animal learns to respond in distinctive ways to his master's commands or other discriminated stimulations.

The primitive sense of similarity that underlies such learning has, we saw, a certain complexity of structure: a is more similar to b than to c. Some people have thought that it has to be much more complex still: that it depends irreducibly on *respects*, thus similarity in color, similarity in shape, and so on. According to this view, our learning of yellow by ostension would have depended on our first having been told or somehow apprised that it was going to be a question of color. Now hints of this kind are a great help, and in our learning we often do depend on them. Still one would like to be able to show that a single general standard of similarity, but of course comparative similarity, is all we need, and that respects can be abstracted afterward. For instance, suppose the child has learned of a yellow ball and block that they count as yellow, and of a red ball and block that they do not, and now he has to decide about a yellow cloth. Presumably he will find the cloth more similar to the yellow ball and to the yellow block than to the red ball or red block; and he will not have needed any prior schooling in colors and respects. Carnap undertook to show long ago how some respects, such as color, could by an ingenious construction be derived from a general similarity notion; [8] however, this development is challenged, again, by Goodman's difficulty of imperfect community.

A standard of similarity is in some sense innate. This point is not against empiricism; it is a commonplace of behavioral psychology. A response to a red circle, if it is rewarded, will be elicited again by a pink ellipse more readily than by a blue triangle; the red circle resembles the pink ellipse more than the blue triangle. Without some such prior spacing of qualities, we could never acquire a habit; all stimuli would be equally alike and equally different. These spacings of qualities, on the part of men and other animals, can be explored and mapped in the laboratory by experiments in conditioning and extinction. [9] Needed as they are for all learning, these distinctive spacings cannot themselves all be learned; some must be innate.

If then I say that there is an innate standard of similarity, I am making a condensed statement that can be interpreted, and truly interpreted, in behavioral terms. Moreover, in this behavioral sense it can be said equally of other animals that they have an innate standard of similarity too. It is part of our animal birthright. And, interestingly enough, it is characteristically animal in its lack of intellectual status. At any rate we noticed earlier how alien the notion is to mathematics and logic.

This innate qualitative spacing of stimulations was seen to have one of its human uses in the ostensive learning of words like "yellow." I should add as a cautionary remark that this is not the only way of learning words, nor the commonest; it is

[8] Rudolf Carnap, *The Logical Structure of the World* (California, 1967), pp. 141–147. (German edition 1928).

[9] See my *Word and Object*, pp. 83 f, for further discussion and references.

merely the most rudimentary way. It works when the question of the reference of a word is a simple question of spread: how much of our surroundings counts as yellow, how much counts as water, and so on. Learning a word like "apple" or "square" is more complicated, because here we have to learn also where to say that one apple or square leaves off and another begins. The complication is that apples do not add up to an apple, nor squares, generally, to a square. "Yellow" and "water" are mass terms, concerned only with spread; "apple" and "square" are terms of divided reference, concerned with both spread and individuation. Ostension figures in the learning of terms of this latter kind too, but the process is more complex.[10] And then there are all the other sorts of words, all those abstract and neutral connectives and adverbs and all the recondite terms of scientific theory; and there are also the grammatical constructions themselves to be mastered. The learning of these things is less direct and more complex still. There are deep problems in this domain, but they lie aside from the present topic.

Our way of learning "yellow," then, gives less than a full picture of how we learn language. Yet more emphatically, it gives less than a full picture of the human use of an innate standard of similarity, or innate spacing of qualities. For, as remarked, every reasonable expectation depends on similarity. Again on this score, other animals are like man. Their expectations, if we choose so to conceptualize their avoidance movements and salivation and pressing of levers and the like, are clearly dependent on their appreciation of similarity. Or, to put matters in their methodological order, these avoidance movements and salivation and pressing of levers and the like are typical of what we have to go on in mapping the animals' appreciation of similarity, their spacing of qualities.

[10] See *Word and Object*, pp. 90-95.

Induction itself is essentially only more of the same: animal expectation or habit formation. And the ostensive learning of words is an implicit case of induction. Implicitly the learner of "yellow" is working inductively toward a general law of English verbal behavior, though a law that he will never try to state; he is working up to where he can in general judge when an English speaker would assent to "yellow" and when not.

Not only is ostensive learning a case of induction; it is a curiously comfortable case of induction, a game of chance with loaded dice. At any rate this is so if, as seems plausible, each man's spacing of qualities is enough like his neighbor's. For the learner is generalizing on his yellow samples by similarity considerations, and his neighbors have themselves acquired the use of the word "yellow", in their day, by the same similarity considerations. The learner of "yellow" is thus making his induction in a friendly world. Always, induction expresses our hope that similar causes will have similar effects; but when the induction is the ostensive learning of a word, that pious hope blossoms into a foregone conclusion. The uniformity of people's quality spaces virtually assures that similar presentations will elicit similar verdicts.

It makes one wonder the more about other inductions, where what is sought is a generalization not about our neighbor's verbal behavior but about the harsh impersonal world. It is reasonable that our quality space should match our neighbor's, we being birds of a feather; and so the general trustworthiness of induction in the ostensive learning of words was a put-up job. To trust induction as a way of access to the truths of nature, on the other hand, is to suppose, more nearly, that our quality space matches that of the cosmos. The brute irrationality of our sense of similarity, its irrelevance to anything in logic and mathematics, offers little reason to expect that this sense is somehow in tune with the world—a world which, unlike language, we never made. Why induction should be trusted, apart from special cases such as the ostensive learning of words, is the perennial philosophical problem of induction.

One part of the problem of induction, the part that asks why there should be regularities in nature at all, can, I think, be dismissed. *That* there are or have been regularities, for whatever reason, is an established fact of science; and we cannot ask better than that. *Why* there have been regularities is an obscure question, for it is hard to see what would count as an answer. What does make clear sense is this other part of the problem of induction: why does our innate subjective spacing of qualities accord so well with the functionally relevant groupings in nature as to make our inductions tend to come out right? Why should our subjective spacing of qualities have a special purchase on nature and a lien on the future?

There is some encouragement in Darwin. If people's innate spacing of qualities is a gene-linked trait, then the spacing that has made for the most successful inductions will have tended to predominate through natural selection.[11] Creatures inveterately wrong in their inductions have a pathetic but praiseworthy tendency to die before reproducing their kind.

At this point let me say that I shall not be impressed by protests that I am using inductive generalizations, Darwin's and others, to justify induction, and thus reasoning in a circle. The reason I shall not be impressed by this is that my position is a naturalistic one; I see philosophy not as an *a priori* propaedeutic or groundwork for science, but as continuous with science. I

[11] This was noted by S. Watanabe on the second page of his paper "Une explication mathématique du classement d'objets," in S. Dockx and P. Bernays, eds., *Information and Prediction in Science* (New York: Academy Press, 1965).

see philosophy and science as in the same boat—a boat which, to revert to Neurath's figure as I so often do, we can rebuild only at sea while staying afloat in it. There is no external vantage point, no first philosophy. All scientific findings, all scientific conjectures that are at present plausible, are therefore in my view as welcome for use in philosophy as elsewhere. For me then the problem of induction is a problem about the world: a problem of how we, as we now are (by our present scientific lights), in a world we never made, should stand better than random or coin-tossing chances of coming out right when we predict by inductions which are based on our innate, scientifically unjustified similarity standard. Darwin's natural selection is a plausible partial explanation.

It may, in view of a consideration to which I next turn, be almost explanation enough. This consideration is that induction, after all, has its conspicuous failures. Thus take color. Nothing in experience, surely, is more vivid and conspicuous than color and its contrasts. And the remarkable fact, which has impressed scientists and philosophers as far back at least as Galileo and Descartes, is that the distinctions that matter for basic physical theory are mostly independent of color contrasts. Color impresses man; raven black impresses Hempel; emerald green impresses Goodman. But color is cosmically secondary. Even slight differences in sensory mechanisms from species to species, Smart remarks,[12] can make overwhelming differences in the grouping of things by color. Color is king in our innate quality space, but undistinguished in cosmic circles. Cosmically, colors would not qualify as kinds.

Color is helpful at the food-gathering level. Here it behaves

[12] J. J. C. Smart, *Philosophy and Scientific Realism* (New York: Humanities, 1963), pp. 68–72.

well under induction, and here, no doubt, has been the survival value of our color-slanted quality space. It is just that contrasts that are crucial for such activities can be insignificant for broader and more theoretical science. If man were to live by basic science alone, natural selection would shift its support to the color-blind mutation.

Living as he does by bread and basic science both, man is torn. Things about his innate similarity sense that are helpful in the one sphere can be a hindrance in the other. Credit is due man's inveterate ingenuity, or human sapience, for having worked around the blinding dazzle of color vision and found the more significant regularities elsewhere. Evidently natural selection has dealt with the conflict by endowing man doubly: with both a color-slanted quality space and the ingenuity to rise above it.

He has risen above it by developing modified systems of kinds, hence modified similarity standards for scientific purposes. By the trial-and-error process of theorizing he has regrouped things into new kinds which prove to lend themselves to many inductions better than the old.

A crude example is the modification of the notion of fish by excluding whales and porpoises. Another taxonomic example is the grouping of kangaroos, opossums, and marsupial mice in a single kind, marsupials, while excluding ordinary mice. By primitive standards the marsupial mouse is more similar to the ordinary mouse than to the kangaroo; by theoretical standards the reverse is true.

A theoretical kind need not be a modification of an intuitive one. It may issue from theory full-blown, without antecedents; for instance the kind which comprises positively charged particles.

We revise our standards of similarity or of natural kinds on the strength, as Goodman remarks,[13] of second-order inductions. New groupings, hypothetically adopted at the suggestion of a growing theory, prove favorable to inductions and so become "entrenched." We newly establish the projectibility of some predicate, to our satisfaction, by successfully trying to project it. In induction nothing succeeds like success.

Between an innate similarity notion or spacing of qualities and a scientifically sophisticated one, there are all gradations. Sciences, after all, differs from common sense only in degree of methodological sophistication. Our experiences from earliest infancy are bound to have overlaid our innate spacing of qualities by modifying and supplementing our grouping habits little by little, inclining us more and more to an appreciation of theoretical kinds and similarities, long before we reach the point of studying science systematically as such. Moreover, the later phases do not wholly supersede the earlier; we retain different similarity standards, different systems of kinds, for use in different contexts. We all still say that a marsupial mouse is more like an ordinary mouse than a kangaroo, except when we are concerned with genetic matters. Something like our innate quality space continues to function alongside the more sophisticated regroupings that have been found by scientific experience to facilitate induction.

We have seen that a sense of similarity or of kinds is fundamental to learning in the widest sense—to language learning, to induction, to expectation. Toward a further appreciation of how utterly this notion permeates our thought, I want now to point out a number of other very familiar and central notions which seem to depend squarely on this one. They are notions that are definable in terms of similarity, or kinds, and further irreducible.

[13] Goodman, *Fact*, pp. 95 ff.

A notable domain of examples is the domain of dispositions, such as Carnap's example of solubility in water. To say of some individual object that it is soluble in water is not to say merely that it always dissolves when in water, because this would be true by default of any object, however insoluble, if it merely happened to be destined never to get into water. It is to say rather that it *would* dissolve if it were in water; but this account brings small comfort, since the device of a subjunctive conditional involves all the perplexities of disposition terms and more. Thus far I simply repeat Carnap.[14] But now I want to point out what could be done in this connection with the notion of kind. Intuitively, what qualifies a thing as soluble though it never gets into water is that it is of the same kind as the things that actually did or will dissolve; it is similar to them. Strictly we can't simply say *"the* same kind," nor simply "similar," when we have wider and narrower kinds, less and more similarity. Let us then mend our definition by saying that the soluble things are the common members of *all* such kinds. A thing is soluble if *each* kind that is broad enough to embrace all actual victims of solution embraces it too.

Graphically the idea is this: we make a set of all the some-time victims, all the things that actually did or will dissolve in water, and then we add just enough other things to round the set out into a kind. This is the water-soluble kind.

If this definition covers just the desired things, the things that are really soluble in water, it owes its success to a circumstance that could be otherwise. The needed circumstance is that a sufficient variety of things actually get dissolved in water to assure their not all falling under any one kind narrower than the desired water-soluble kind itself. But it is a plausible cir-

[14] Carnap, "Testability and meaning," *Philosophy of Science* 3 (1936), 419–471; 4 (1937), 1–40.

cumstance, and I am not sure that its accidental character is a drawback. If the trend of events had been otherwise, perhaps the solubility concept would not have been wanted.

However, if I seem to be defending this definition, I must now hasten to add that of course it has much the same fault as the definition which used the subjunctive conditional. This definition uses the unreduced notion of kind, which is certainly not a notion we want to rest with either; neither theoretical kind nor intuitive kind. My purpose in giving the definition is only to show the link between the problem of dispositions and the problem of kinds.

As between theoretical and intuitive kinds, certainly the theoretical ones are the ones wanted for purposes of defining solubility and other dispositions of scientific concern. Perhaps "amiable" and "reprehensible" are disposition terms whose definitions should draw rather on intuitive kinds.

In considering the disposition of solubility we observed a link first with the subjunctive conditional and then with the notion of kind. This suggests comparing also the two end terms, so as to see the connection between the subjunctive conditional and the notion of kind. We had then, on the one side, the subjunctive conditional "If x were in water it would dissolve"; and on the other side, in terms of kinds, we had "Each kind that embraces all things that ever get into water and dissolve, embraces x." Here we have equated a sample subjunctive conditional to a sentence about kinds. We can easily enough generalize the equivalence to cover a significant class of subjunctive conditionals: the form "If x were an F then x would be a G" gets equated to "Each kind that embraces all Fs that are Gs embraces x." Notice that the Fs themselves, here, would not be expected to constitute a kind; nor the Gs; nor the Fs which are Gs. But you take the fewest things you can which, added to the Fs which are Gs, suffice to round the set out to a kind. Then x is one of these few additional things; this is the interpretation we get of the subjunctive conditional "If x were an F then x would be a G."

One might try this formula out on other examples, and study it for possible light on subjunctive conditionals more generally. Some further insight into this queer idiom might thus be gained. But let us remember that we are still making uncritical use of the unreduced notion of kind. My purpose, again, is only to show the link between these matters.

Another dim notion, which has intimate connections with dispositions and subjunctive conditionals, is the notion of cause; and we shall see that it too turns on the notion of kinds. Hume explained cause as invariable succession, and this makes sense as long as the cause and effect are referred to by general terms. We can say that fire causes heat, and we can mean thereby, as Hume would have it, that each event classifiable under the head of fire is followed by an event classifiable under the head of heat, or heating up. But this account, whatever its virtues for these general causal statements, leaves singular causal statements unexplained.

What does it mean to say that the kicking over of a lamp in Mrs. Leary's barn caused the Chicago fire? It cannot mean merely that the event at Mrs. Leary's belongs to a set, and the Chicago fire belongs to a set, such that there is invariable succession between the two sets: every member of the one set is followed by a member of the other. This paraphrase is trivially true and too weak. Always, if one event happens to be followed by another, the two belong to *certain* sets between which there is invariable succession. We can rig the sets arbitrarily. Just put any arbitrary events in the first set, including the first of the two events we are interested in; and then in the other set put the second of those two events, together with other events that happen to have occurred just after the other members of the first set.

Because of this way of trivialization, a singular causal statement says no more than that the one event was followed by the other. That is, it says no more if we use the definition just now contemplated; which, therefore, we must not. The trouble with that definition is clear enough: it is the familiar old trouble of the promiscuity of sets. Here, as usual, kinds, being more discriminate, enable us to draw distinctions where sets do not. To say that one event caused another is to say that the two events are of *kinds* between which there is invariable succession. If this correction does not yet take care of Mrs. Leary's cow, the fault is only with invariable succession itself, as affording too simple a definition of general causal statements; we need to hedge it around with provisions for partial or contributing causes and a good deal else. That aspect of the causality problem is not my concern. What I wanted to bring out is just the relevance of the notion of kinds, as the needed link between singular and general causal statements.

We have noticed that the notion of kind, or similarity, is crucially relevant to the notion of disposition, to the subjunctive conditional, and to singular causal statements. From a scientific point of view these are a pretty disreputable lot. The notion of kind, or similarity, is equally disreputable. Yet some such notion, some similarity sense, was seen to be crucial to all learning, and central in particular to the processes of inductive generalization and prediction which are the very life of science. It appears that science is rotten to the core.

Yet there may be claimed for this rot a certain undeniable fecundity. Science reveals hidden mysteries, predicts successfully, and works technological wonders. If this is the way of rot, then rot is rather to be prized and praised than patronized.

Rot, actually, is not the best model here. A better model is human progress. A sense of comparative similarity, I remarked earlier, is one of man's animal endowments. Insofar as it fits in with regularities of nature, so as to afford us reasonable success in our primitive inductions and expectations, it is presumably an evolutionary product of natural selection. Secondly, as remarked, one's sense of similarity or one's system of kinds develops and changes and even turns multiple as one matures, making perhaps for increasingly dependable prediction. And at length standards of similarity set in which are geared to theoretical science. This development is a development away from the immediate, subjective, animal sense of similarity to the remoter objectivity of a similarity determined by scientific hypotheses and posits and constructs. Things are similar in the later or theoretical sense to the degree that they are interchangeable parts of the cosmic machine revealed by science.

This progress of similarity standards, in the course of each individual's maturing years, is a sort of recapitulation in the individual of the race's progress from muddy savagery. But the similarity notion even in its theoretical phase is itself a muddy notion still. We have offered no definition of it in satisfactory scientific terms. We of course have a behavioral definition of what counts, for a given individual, as similar to what, or as more similar to what than to what; we have this for similarity old and new, human and animal. But it is no definition of what it means really for a to be more similar to b than to c; really, and quite apart from this or that psychological subject.

Did I already suggest a definition to this purpose, metaphorically, when I said that things are similar to the extent that they are interchangeable parts of the cosmic machine? More literally, could things be said to be similar in proportion to how much of scientific theory would remain true on interchanging those things as objects of reference in the theory? This only hints a direction; consider for instance the dimness of "how much theory." Anyway the direction itself is not a good one; for it would make similarity depend in the wrong way on theory. A man's judgments of similarity do and should depend on his theory, on his beliefs; but similarity itself, what the man's judgments purport to be judgments of, purports to be an objective relation in the world. It belongs in the subject matter not of our theory of theorizing about the world, but of our theory of the world itself. Such would be the acceptable and reputable sort of similarity concept, if it could be defined.

It does get defined in bits: bits suited to special branches of science. In this way, on many limited fronts, man continues his rise from savagery, sloughing off the muddy old notion of kind or similarity piecemeal, a vestige here and a vestige there. Chemistry, the home science of water-solubility itself, is one branch that has reached this stage. Comparative similarity of the sort that matters for chemistry can be stated outright in chemical terms, that is, in terms of chemical composition. Molecules will be said to *match* if they contain atoms of the same elements in the same topological combinations. Then, in principle, we might get at the comparative similarity of objects a and b by considering how many pairs of matching molecules there are, one molecule from a and one from b each time, and how many unmatching pairs. The ratio gives even a theoretical measure of relative similarity, and thus abundantly explains what it is for a to be more similar to b than to c. Or we might prefer to complicate our definition by allowing also for degrees in the matching of molecules; molecules having almost equally many atoms, or having atoms whose atomic numbers or atomic weights are almost equal, could be reckoned as matching better than others. At any rate a lusty chemical similarity concept is assured.

From it, moreover, an equally acceptable concept of kinds is derivable, by the paradigm-and-foil definition noted early in this paper. For it is a question now only of distilling purely chemical kinds from purely chemical similarity; no admixture of other respects of similarity interferes. We thus exonerate water-solubility, which, the last time around, we had reduced no further than to an unexplained notion of kind. Therewith also the associated subjunctive conditional, "If this were in water it would dissolve," gets its bill of health.

The same scientific advances that have thus provided a solid underpinning for the definition of solubility in terms of kinds, have also, ironically enough, made that line of definition pointless by providing a full understanding of the mechanism of solution. One can redefine water-solubility by simply describing the structural conditions of that mechanism. This embarrassment of riches is, I suspect, a characteristic outcome. That is, once we can legitimize a disposition term by defining the relevant similarity standard, we are apt to know the mechanism of the disposition, and so by-pass the similarity. Not but that the similarity standard is worth clarifying too, for its own sake or for other purposes.

Philosophical or broadly scientific motives can impel us to seek still a basic and absolute concept of similarity, along with such fragmentary similarity concepts as suit special branches of science. This drive for a cosmic similarity concept is perhaps identifiable with the age-old drive to reduce things to their elements. It epitomizes the scientific spirit, though dating back to the pre-Socratics: to Empedocles with his theory of four elements, and above all to Democritus with his atoms. The modern physics of elementary particles, or of hills in space-time, is a more notable effort in this direction.

This idea of rationalizing a single notion of relative similarity, throughout its cosmic sweep, has its metaphysical attractions. But there would remain still need also to rationalize the similarity notion more locally and superficially, so as to capture only such similarity as is relevant to some special science. Our chemistry example is already a case of this, since it stops short of full analysis into neutrons, electrons, and the other elementary particles.

A more striking example of superficiality, in this good sense, is afforded by taxonomy, say in zoology. Since learning about the evolution of species, we are in a position to define comparative similarity suitably for this science by consideration of family trees. For a theoretical measure of the degree of similarity of two individual animals we can devise some suitable function that depends on proximity and frequency of their common ancestors. Or a more significant concept of degree of similarity might be devised in terms of genes. When kind is construed in terms of any such similarity concept, fishes in the corrected, whale-free sense of the word qualify as a kind while fishes in the more inclusive sense do not.

Different similarity measures, or relative similarity notions, best suit different branches of science; for there are wasteful complications in providing for finer gradations of relative similarity than matter for the phenomena with which the particular science is concerned. Perhaps the branches of science could be revealingly classified by looking to the relative similarity notion that is appropriate to each. Such a plan is reminiscent of Felix Klein's so-called *Erlangerprogramm* in geometry, which involved characterizing the various branches of geometry by what transformations were irrelevant to each. But a branch of science would only qualify for recognition and classification under such a plan when it had matured to the point of clearing up its similarity notion. Such branches of science would qualify further as unified, or integrated into our inclusive systematization of nature, only insofar as their several similarity concepts were *compatible;* capable of meshing, that is, and differing only in the fineness of their discriminations.

Disposition terms and subjunctive conditionals in these areas, where suitable senses of similarity and kind are forthcoming, suddenly turn respectable; respectable and, in principle, superfluous. In other domains they remain disreputable and practically indispensable. They may be seen perhaps as unredeemed notes; the theory that would clear up the unanalyzed underlying similarity notion in such cases is still to come. An example is the disposition called intelligence—the ability, vaguely speaking, to learn quickly and to solve problems. Sometime, whether in terms of proteins or colloids or nerve nets or overt behavior, the relevant branch of science may reach the stage where a similarity notion can be constructed capable of making even the notion of intelligence respectable. And superfluous.

In general we can take it as a very special mark of the maturity of a branch of science that it no longer needs an irreducible notion of similarity and kind. It is that final stage where the animal vestige is wholly absorbed into the theory. In this career of the similarity notion, starting in its innate phase, developing over the years in the light of accumulated experience, passing then from the intuitive phase into theoretical similarity, and finally disappearing altogether, we have a paradigm of the evolution of unreason into science.

6

Propositional
Objects

A declarative sentence is usually true or false. But your typical declarative sentence is not fixedly true or false. It is true on one occasion and false on another, because of the tenses of its verbs and the varying references of its pronouns or demonstrative adverbs or other indicator words. By incorporating additional information into the sentence, such as dates and the names of persons and places, we can obtain an *eternal sentence:* one that is fixedly true or false. Thus an eternal sentence need not be a law of mathematics or of nature; it can also be a report of a passing event.

Now a *proposition* is the meaning of a sentence. More precisely, since propositions are supposed to be true or false once and for all, a proposition is the meaning of an eternal sentence. More precisely still, it is the *cognitive* meaning of an eternal sentence; that is, just so much of the meaning as affects the truth value of the sentence and not its poetic quality or its affective tone.

Not that *this* is precise. The word "meaning" survives in my explanation, and it covers a multitude of sins. When I explain propositions as the cognitive meanings of eternal sentences, I am merely telling you which of various unsatisfactory notions it is that I am going to be worrying about.

I shall speak of why the notion of proposition or something like it seems to be wanted, and I shall speak of obstacles to rendering it satisfactory. Also I shall bring up other notions somewhat akin to that of proposition, and consider whether these might do some of the work for which propositions had been wanted. It is because of these other notions that instead of giving my subject simply as "Propositions" I have given it yet more vaguely as "Propositional Objects." I mean the term to apply to any of the things that might be proposed as meanings of sentences or as objects of the propositional attitudes.

The trouble with propositions, as the cognitive meanings of eternal sentences, is individuation. Given two eternal sentences, themselves visibly different as linguistic forms, it is not sufficiently clear under what circumstances to say that they mean the same proposition. It is on this score that the sentences are less dubious entities than the propositions.

L. J. Cohen sees matters differently. He is prepared to accept meanings in one or another sense to play propositional roles, but he is not prepared to recognize eternal sentences for them to be meanings of. "No language-sentence whatever can be relied on to maintain its truth-value invariant under all circumstances," he writes.[1] What he is worried about is semantic change in language from time to time or from speaker to speaker. We cannot disallow this factor by stipulating that sameness of language is intended, because, he says, when word forms are the same, there is no saying what to count as doctrinal disagreement and what to count as linguistic disagreement.

[1] L. J. Cohen, *The Diversity of Meaning* (London: Methuen, 1962), p. 232.

Now I can sympathize with this remark, but let us see just how it bears on the notion of eternal sentence. It bears certainly on whether a sentence can be relied on to remain *accepted* as true. A man may change his verdict, and we may not know whether to account this a change of language in the given case. But truth value is not verdict. The semantics of truth is linked to verbal behavior only less directly. When a man changes his verdict on an eternal sentence, now denying it, say, the significant thing is that he will hold also that the sentence always was really false; he will not say that his earlier verdict was right too and this is just a different case. He may say he has changed his mind, or he may doubt having made the earlier verdict, or he may say he has changed his language, that is, that he is using a word differently.

The subtlety of the matter can be brought out by reflecting that a sentence may even be an eternal sentence for a speaker at one time and not at another. Maybe someone can devise a natural example of this. It *would* have to be a case of linguistic change. And it would still be right to say of the sentence, on the earlier occasion, that it is true forever or false forever. *Qua* sentence of that language, of course.

Cohen could rightly say, then, that whether a sentence is eternal depends on what language you are thinking of it as a sentence of. If there is a language in which the form of words "It is raining" means "Iron is a metal," then "It is raining" is an eternal sentence for that language and not for English. But this brand of relativity applies to mere truth as well as to eternality. We all know that truth values, applied to sentences, depend on a language parameter; a sentence may by phonetic accident be true here and now as a sentence of one language and false here and now as a sentence of another. The notion of an eternal sentence is only as badly off as the notion of a sentence's being true here and now. But this, I must say, is bad enough. I dislike imagining a tacit subscript on the word "true," or "eternal," specifying the language. A trouble with the notion of a language is that it, like the very notion of proposition or meaning that I have complained about, has been given no satisfactory principle of individuation.

One use that has been made of propositions, in order to dodge the relativity to language, is as truth vehicles: propositions, it is said, and not sentences are what are true or false. But it seems exorbitant to posit propositions for this purpose. Being true or false does not depend on how propositions are individuated, after all, and yet the notion of proposition itself does. In *Word and Object* (p. 208), consequently, I favored taking the eternal sentences themselves as the truth vehicles. They are better than other sentences, at any rate, as being true or false independently of time, place, speaker, and the like. But they are as bad as other sentences in admitting of variation in truth value from one language to another.

To resort to propositions for the purpose of truth vehicles does not solve the problem, however; it merely gives up on it.

Another alternative to consider, as truth vehicle, is the concrete event of utterance. I wonder whether we can agree that no such event is bilingual, even when the speaker is bilingual and the form of words belongs by coincidence to both his languages and has opposite truth values in the two. It may be felt that to concede this is to assume covertly an unanalyzed distinction between meanings in the speaker's mind, and that we could as well accept those meanings as propositions and be done with it. At any rate Scheffler has used utterance events, not as truth vehicles but as objects of propositional attitudes, in the belief that he thus avoided the language-identification problem.[2]

[2] "An inscriptional approach to indirect quotation," *Analysis* 14 (1954), 83–90.

I suppose the thing to do is to look upon that infinitely rare bilingual coincidence simply as an ambiguous utterance. So the plan I now propose is to take as truth vehicles not eternal sentences but eternal-sentence utterance events: utterances of sentences that are eternal sentences for the utterer at the time; or, to revert to language language, utterances of sentences that are eternal sentences of the language that the utterer is speaking at the time.

But utterance events present a new difficulty as truth vehicles: the difficulty that only a finite and therefore infinitesimal proportion of our sentences ever get uttered, even if we count writing as uttering. Such laws as that any two falsehoods form a false alternation, and any two truths form a true conjunction, become hard to construe if the existence of utterances matters. We would seem driven at that point to contrary-to-fact conditionals, and thus out of the frying pan into the fire. It is a difficulty that did not arise as long as we talked of sentences, linguistic forms rather than of utterance events, because a sentence can be thought of as simply the sequence, not in the historical but in the mathematical sense, of its successive letters or phonemes. Sentences in this sense will always exist, regardless of utterance, and not vacuously as the null class, either, if we allow a modicum of set theory.

What, then, to do about utterance events as truth vehicles? I have two ideas. The first one is that we explain existing logical theory as a convenient schematism that can be applied to give right results when suitable existence conditions in respect of utterances happen to be met. This idea would take some working out. The second idea is that we let the truth vehicles be the eternal sentences after all, as they were in *Word and Object,* and then just find a way of tolerating the tacit dependence of truth and eternality upon a language parameter.

I suggest that we assign to that parameter, as its value, the language that the speaker is speaking when his tacit use of the parameter takes place. This ego-directed parameter does not really raise the general problem of individuation of languages, though my use of the word "language" would seem to raise it. For it is enough that the speaker's own total present speech dispositions be taken as the value of the parameter.

Dispositions. Out of the frying pan into the fire again? I think not. We are always involved in talk of dispositions, even in the most empirical studies of speech behavior and of natural phenomena generally. A disposition to do a certain thing when stimulated in a certain way is a mechanism, already mechanically understood or not, in the organism; and the name of the disposition tells us how to gather evidence of varying conclusiveness for its presence. We cannot gather much evidence at a given moment for a speaker's range of speech dispositions at that moment, true. But we can gather, for his dispositions at a moment, much evidence at other moments: indirect evidence from which we reason according to plausible psychological theories and generalizations regarding the persistence of habits and other matters.

So much for propositions as truth vehicles. Now another purpose for which propositions have long been thought to be needed is as objects of the propositional attitudes of believing, wishing, striving, regretting, and the like. Here the individuation problem is acute. We quote a man's previously enunciated belief in our own words; what changes of phrasing will have made a different belief of it, perhaps falsifying our imputation of it to him? Here an over-fine individuation would do no harm; we would merely get excessively discriminated beliefs moving in bundles. But an over-coarse individuation would be harmful. As for other contexts, some are sensitive in both directions. For instance, suppose I say I have given up precisely three beliefs since lunch. An over-coarse individuation could reduce the number to two, and an over-fine one could raise it to four.

It is conceivable, for that matter, that different principles of individuation, hence different senses of "proposition," might be wanted for different propositional attitudes. An individuation of propositions that is proposed in some philosophical connections makes sentences mean identical propositions when and only when the biconditional of the sentences is analytic; and this does seem to be too coarse an individuation for the purposes of a theory of belief. But I am speaking impressionistically, for there is not to my knowledge an acceptably clear notion of analyticity, let alone an individuation of beliefs.

A discouraging thing about the propositional attitudes is that the very obstacles to a satisfactory individuation of their objects are obstacles also to a clear interpretation of the idioms of propositional attitude even apart from their objects. Thus take belief. If I repudiate beliefs as objects, I give up saying things like "I have stopped believing something (or three things) since lunch." I can still profess and impute beliefs explicitly, one by one. I can still say that I believe that the faces of the Great Pyramid are equilateral; this I can say even though denying that there are any such things as *that* the faces of the pyramid are equilateral, along with there being such things as I and the pyramid and its faces. But in repudiating beliefs as objects what do I gain? The problem whether, in believing the faces equilateral, I *ipso facto* believe them equiangular, is of a piece with the individuation problem and it is still there to confront us when the beliefs as objects are dropped.

In *Word and Object* (p. 218), I suggest that the question how far we can rephrase a belief, and not lose the right to impute it, depends on our purpose in imputing it. Correspondingly for propositional attitudes other than belief. This being the case, there is no hope of a general translation of the idioms of propositional attitude into other and more objective terms. In each particular case, knowing the circumstances, we may be able to say something in other terms that would be no less useful as an aid to transacting some business in hand; but we can hope for no verbal equivalent of "a believes that p," even for given "a" and "p," that is independent of the circumstances under which it may have been said that a believes that p. The situation is like that of indicator words: You cannot eliminate indicator words by paraphrasing a sentence without regard to the date or other circumstances of its utterance. So in *Word and Object* (p. 221) I left the idioms of propositional attitude in a second-grade status, along with the indicator words: the status of useful vernacular having no place in the austere apparatus of scientific theory.

I think none of us is uncomfortable about relegating the indicator words to that status, despite their utility. We understand both why they are useful and why they would bring no enrichment to the vocabulary of scientific law. We can foresee how in each particular situation we would set about circumventing an indicator word. Over relegating the idioms of propositional attitude, however, one is less comfortable. One has a sense of genuine loss.

We like to say for instance that the cat wants to get on to the roof, or is afraid the dog will hurt him. In so saying we purport to relate the cat perhaps to a state of affairs. The cat wants, or fears, the state of affairs. His wanting or fearing is a strictly physiological affair, granted, and our evidence for it is our observation of the cat's overt behavior. But the particular range of possible physiological states, each of which would count as a case of wanting to get on to that particular roof, is a gerry-mandered range of states that could surely not be encapsulated in any manageable anatomical description even if we knew all about cats. Again the range of possible sequences of overt behavior, each of which would count as evidence of wanting to get on to that particular roof, is a gerrymandered range that cannot be encapsulated in any compact behavioral description. Relations to states of affairs, such relations as wanting and fearing, afford some very special and seemingly indispensable ways of grouping events in the natural world.

Our philosophical difficulties over them have perhaps arisen in part from the *sentential* bias of our idioms of propositional attitude. These idioms all follow the pattern of indirect quotation, and so involve us in the problem of limits of allowable variation of the subordinate sentence. Such a textual problem seems ludicrously irrelevant when we come to dumb animals; what the cat wants is a simple matter of superposition with respect to the roof, by whatever name. Can we perhaps accommodate some primitive cases, at least, of the propositional attitudes by talking of states of affairs, in some sense of the term very unlike the idea of proposition or of sentence?

Let us begin by thinking of a state of affairs as a class of possible worlds: the class of all the possible worlds in which, intuitively speaking, that state of affairs would be realized. What then is a possible world? To simplify matters let us accept for a while an old-fashioned physics according to which, as Democritus held, all atoms are homogeneous in substance and differ only in size, shape, position, and motion. Let us suppose further that space is Euclidean.

Now when this much is granted, there remain for each point in space just two possible states: the point may lie within some particle or it may be empty. Each distribution of these states over all the points of space may be seen, not yet quite as a possible world, but as a possible momentary world state.

It is somewhat as if we were taking possible world states as state descriptions in Carnap's sense, and taking our sole predicate as the predicate "occupied," and taking our individual constants as the names of the points of space. But this is not quite it. One objection to state descriptions is that each individual would have to have a name. Our individuals are here the points of space and we know that they are not all nameable, since they are indenumerable while names are denumerable. The virtue of taking a possible world state as an exhaustive assignment of "occupied" or "empty," "yes" or "no," to points of space, is that the assignment does not have to be seen as a state description; it does not have to be verbal. It can simply be identified with the aggregate of the occupied points themselves. Each portion of space, big or little, compact or scattered, may thus be accounted a possible world state. Realization of that world state would consist in there being matter at each of those points of space and none elsewhere.

What are points, though, and what is space? Would we be committed to two sorts of individuals, namely points of space and portions of matter? No, we can by-pass the points by adopting a system of coordinates and speaking of triples of real numbers. Our ontology then requires only portions of matter, as individuals, and the usual superstructure of classes of individuals, classes of such classes, and so on. The real numbers find their place in the third or fourth story of this edifice, as is well known.

On this approach, a possible world state becomes simply any class of triples of real numbers. To any such class we equate what, intuitively, would be called the possible world state that has matter at just the positions given by number triples in the class.

I passed over a compelling reason for shifting from points to number triples. There is the desire for ontological economy; there is the puzzle over just what a point might otherwise be; but also, and more compellingly, there is the relativity of position. Unless we are prepared to believe that absolute position makes sense, the very idea of a point as an entity in its own right must be rejected as not merely mysterious but absurd. And notice that I am not speaking of Einstein's relativity here; I am speaking of Leibniz's.

Actually a problem of relativity of position is still with us when we give up the points in favor of the number triples. The assigning of numbers depends on an arbitrary choice of coordinates; this would be arbitrary even if position itself were absolute. A possible world state should continue to be the same possible world state when we shift or rotate the coordinate axes; yet this changes the number triples.

The version of a possible world state as a class of number triples is thus still in trouble. But we can rise above the trouble by ascending one more level and taking a possible world state rather as a class of classes of number triples. Instead of taking it as a particular class C of triples we take it as the class of all the classes into which C could be carried by translation and rotation of coordinate axes. Described figuratively in terms of points again instead of triples, what has happened is that instead of taking a possible world state as a point set we are taking it as the class of all point sets congruent to a given point set.

We have thus risen above the arbitrariness of position and orientation of coordinate axes. That much, I remarked, would have been arbitrary even if position itself were absolute. But

note now that our correction has in fact achieved the desired
relativity on both counts. In abstracting from differences of coordinate axes it leaves no way whereby we could mark absolute positions if we wanted to. Happily we do not want to. If
we believed in absolute space we should have had, perhaps, to
accept some still admittedly arbitrary system of coordinates to
go with it.

As it is, our new possible world states are free of all taint of
absolute place and of arbitrary coordinates. Arbitrariness, even
so, remains in another quarter: the arbitrariness of the units
for measuring distance. Switching from feet to inches has the
effect of multiplying all the numbers in our number triples by
twelve, and so changing our possible world state to another, if
a possible world state is a class of classes of number triples as
last conceived; and this is intolerable, since surely a possible
world state should not really be changed by describing it in
inches instead of feet.

We eliminated the previous arbitrariness by taking a possible world state not as a class of triples C, but as the class of all
the classes into which C could be converted by changing the
axes. Now we can eliminate the arbitrariness of unit by further
generalization, taking a possible world state as the class of all
classes into which a class C of triples can be converted by
changing the axes and multiplying all numbers by a constant.
In geometrical language, we are now taking a possible world
state as the class of all the point sets that are geometrically
similar to a given point set; we settle for mere similarity now
instead of congruence.

The previous and lesser step of abstraction, which looked to
congruence, was seen to eliminate not only the arbitrariness of
axes but also any trace of absolute position. Of this we were
glad. Now similarly this new step of abstraction eliminates not

only the arbitrariness of units of measure but also any trace of absolute size. Have we now gone too far? If size is absolute, if it makes sense to speak of a world in which all things are twice as big and twice as far apart as they are in ours, then we have thrown away too much. We have provided for uniform change of all numbers without change of world state; in so doing we made the choice of units immaterial, as desired, but we made absolute size immaterial also apart from units. If this is undesirable, we must perhaps go back and allow some admittedly arbitrary unit of measure after all.

But I am inclined to welcome relativity of size, or distance, as well as that of position. Grant, for instance, that absolute mass plays a role in the actual laws of physics which absolute position does not; still we could declare everywhere a uniform change in absolute mass by making a systematic compensatory change in the laws themselves. The combined maneuver is still of the empty verbal kind that we like to regard as carrying a possible world state only into itself.

Very well, then: a possible world state is any class whose members are all the classes that are geometrically similar to some one class of number triples. For brevity I apply the geometrical predicate directly to the class of number triples; the proper algebraic meaning of it can of course be spelled out.

A possible *world*, finally can be explained in somewhat the same way but with four dimensions, representing space-time. A possible world becomes, roughly, any class whose members are all the classes that are geometrically similar to some one class of number quadruples. But not quite. In one way this is too broad, in another too narrow. It is too broad in that whereas we wanted in the three-dimensional case to allow all rotations of axes, in the four-dimensional case we want the fourth axis, time, to stay untilted. For remember that we are still in pre-Einstein space-time. And it is too narrow in that whereas we wanted in the three-dimensional case to allow all numbers to be changed only by a constant factor, in the four-dimensional case we are content to let the fourth or time coordinate be multiplied by a factor different from that of the other coordinates. The point here is that, being still in pre-Einstein space-time, we are indifferent as to how many feet in space are geometrically equated to a second in time. In short, in passing from the account of possible world states in three dimensions to the account of possible worlds in four dimensions we modify the geometrical-similarity stipulation in these two ways: we strengthen it by requiring that things preserve their polarization with respect to the fourth dimension, and we relax it by permitting a uniform stretching in the fourth dimension.

This explication of possible worlds is predicated on the view that every possible world has homogeneous matter, Euclidean space, and a time dimension independent of frame of reference. These traits, being then traits of all possible worlds, rate as necessary. The view is debatable, since the real world is believed to lack all three traits.

One thing good about this version of possible worlds, nevertheless, is that it stays within a clear extensional ontology. I expect that while still staying within these terms we could complicate it to suit current physics. We might devise a version compatible with current physics and incompatible with worlds of the foregoing sort, or, what would be more difficult still, we might arrive at a version sufficiently broad and neutral to cover the lot. Either outcome would represent a particular decision as to what to count as *possible,* in an extra-logical and somewhat arbitrary sense of the term. But meanwhile I think it will be little strain on our imaginations to imagine that the facts of physics are of the homelier sort to which my detailed version of possible worlds was directed. This is a version that we can easily keep in mind, and it will be no less relevant to the further points I want to make than a more sophisticated version would be.

What the cat wants, then, is the state of affairs that is the class of all possible worlds in which he is on that roof. What he fears is the class of all possible worlds in which the dog has him. What I believe is the class of all possible worlds in which the Great Pyramid has equilateral faces. Another thing I believe is the class of all possible worlds in which Cicero denounced Catiline.

The matter of individuation that had worried us in propositions is satisfactorily settled for states of affairs. The worlds in which the pyramid's faces are equilateral are indeed the worlds in which they are equiangular; not an atom is discrepant. However, there are new troubles. How is Catiline to be identified in the various possible worlds? Must he have been named "Catiline" in each, in order to qualify? How much can his life differ from the real life of Catiline without his ceasing to be our Catiline and having to be seen as another man of that name? Or again, how much can the pyramid differ from the real one? It will have to differ a little in shape, if my belief about it happens in fact to be mistaken. Is it sufficient, for its identification in other worlds, that it have been built by Cheops? How much then can his life differ from the real life of Cheops without his ceasing to be our Cheops?

Even the cat cases are troublesome. In a possible world with many similar cats and dogs and roofs, which cat is to be he? One of these possible worlds will have a cat like him on a roof like his, and another cat like him in the dog's jaws; does it belong to both the desired state of affairs and the feared one?

The cat examples suggest that in abstracting from the particular placement of coordinate axes I went too far. Perhaps we should keep the origin fixed, thus allowing rotation of axes but no shifting of them. The entertainer of the propositional attitude can then be identified as the organism at the origin. This will not take care of the Cicero-Catiline example nor the pyramid example, but it will take care of the cat examples. Each of the possible worlds suited to the cat examples will have its center or origin in the midst of a cat—say at the center of gravity of the cat's pineal gland. The cat will not stay at the spatial origin through all time; that is, he will not cling always to the time axis; but he will be at the spatial origin at time 0, and that will identify him as the cat in the attitude.

What we have now are what we may call *centered* states of affairs. Each is a class of centered possible worlds. Each centered possible world is the class of all the classes of number quadruples that can be got from some one class of number quadruples by multiplying the first three numbers by a constant factor, multiplying the fourth number by a perhaps different constant, and performing the operations that correspond to a rotation of the first three axes. Notice that the time axis stays fixed now; for it was to stay untilted before, and we have now disallowed the shifting of any axes.

So I am suggesting that the objects of propositional attitudes may in some primitive cases, such as the cat examples, be taken as centered states of affairs. This does not cover selfless examples such as the beliefs about Cicero and the pyramid, and whether it may help to open a line of approach to them I cannot say. At any rate the egocentric propositional attitudes, those of wishing or hoping or fearing or trying or expecting *to be* in some sort of physical situation, seem to be the most primitive ones; and they are covered. Perhaps these are the only ones that a dumb animal can reasonably be said to entertain; I expect the others presuppose language.

If we are to deal only with the egocentric propositional attitudes, however, it would seem that even these centered states of affairs take in a lot of unnecessary territory. If the human or feline animal under consideration is attitudinizing strictly about what might hit him, then, instead of taking account of all the possibilities of occupiedness and emptiness on the part of all the points of space-time, we could as well limit our attention to the surface of our self-centered animal and take account merely of the possibilities of activation and inactivation of its several nerve endings. The possibilities in short, of sensory input. We can limit our attentions to the organism, letting the rest of the world go its way, and the organism will be none the wiser. Save the surface and you save all. Activate its surface, scratch its back, and the organism will ask no more.

Instead therefore of a cosmic distribution of binary choices (occupied vs. empty) over the points of space-time, what we have to consider is a distribution of binary choices (activated vs. quiescent) over the sensory receptors of our target animal. Each *such* distribution is a possible world in our new sense— or, as we may better entitle it, a stimulation pattern. Then, instead of taking as object of the propositional attitude a state of affairs in the sense of the range of possible worlds that show the cat on the roof, we can take as object the range of stimulation patterns that go with his being on the roof. Patterns of stimulation of the cat himself.

A range of possible worlds was a state of affairs. What now is a range of stimulation patterns? It is what I called, in *Word and Object,* an affirmative stimulus meaning; or let us just say now a stimulus meaning. In *Word and Object* I talked of stimulus meanings *of* occasion sentences; the stimulus meaning of

"It's raining" is the range of stimulation patterns that would prompt a speaker of the language to assent to "It's raining" if asked. And now these same stimulus meanings—these same ranges of stimulation patterns, though not necessarily allocated to sentences—have turned up as objects of the egocentric propositional attitudes for cats and others.

I like this effect of linking species. After all, the association of an observation sentence with a stimulus meaning is the most primitive phase of language. It is what the infant accomplishes first, in the course of acquiring language, and it is perforce the field linguist's entering wedge into radical translation. Stimulus meanings are there for sentences to mean, some of them, when sentences happen along, and they are there also as objects for the egocentric propositional attitudes, be the attitudinists human or feline. I do not offer any theory of mental imagery applicable to cats or to people. It is just that I am cheered by the hint, however slight, of a common treatment.

See also that we are brought around to something reminiscent of an earlier phase in our considerations. Propositions were thought of as meanings of sentences, and also as the objects of the propositional attitudes. And now here are our stimulus meanings, functioning both as the meanings of some sentences and as the objects of some propositional attitudes. However, stimulus meanings are remote as can be from propositions in the sense of meanings of eternal sentences. They are meanings, on a reasonable usage of "meaning," only of observation sentences.

Whatever may have been felt about relegating idioms of propositional attitudes to a status of second-rate vernacular, we may be sure that some notion of stimulus meaning is needed at the austerest scientific level. If stimulus meanings are good objects for primitive propositional attitudes, then primitive propositional attitudes are assured at last of their objects. For obviously any treatment of language as a natural phenomenon must start with the recognition that certain utterances are keyed to ranges of sensory stimulation patterns; and these ranges are what the stimulus meanings are.

And yet there is, in the detail of the underlying notion of stimulation pattern, a cause for worry. It seems vital that in correlating one subject's verbal behavior with another's, for instance as a basis for translating one language into another, we be able to equate one subject's stimulation to another's. Yet how are we to do so? If we construe stimulation patterns my way, we cannot equate them without supposing homology of receptors; and this is absurd, not only because full homology is implausible, but because it surely ought not to matter.

The problem is stubborn even in computer theory. What does it mean to say that two machines are given the same input? I am speaking here not of a sharing of the input energy, of course, but of full similarity of the two input events for the two machines, where the machines differ. Say we send sixty volts into each machine; does this mean sameness of input? What if in the one machine the first effect of the electricity is to start a motor, and in the other its first effect is to sensitize a photoelectric eye? The question is, in part, how far to pursue the input into the machine and still call it input. And surely there is no answer. In practice we define input for a particular machine in such a way as to simplify our theory of programing that machine; and then we can say what constitutes sameness of input for machines of that model, and not much beyond.

What psychologists have said about stimulation has mostly either been independent of any equating of stimulation from subject to subject, or has involved the equating only of some specific stimulations without raising the general problem. It is when we turn to language theory that the problem becomes acute. Being social, language depends on associating utterances with stimulations that can be publicly identified in their recurrences from occasion to occasion and speaker to speaker.

It is the stimulation at the bodily surface that counts, and not just the objective existence of objects of reference off in the distance, nor yet the events deep inside the body. Even a primitive mother, in encouraging or discouraging a child's use of a word on a given occasion, will consider whether the relevant object is visible from where the child sits. And even a highly civilized mother is content, when checking the child's testimony against the child's data, not to penetrate the child's surface. The bodily surface would thus seem to be, for an activity ever subject to social adjustment as language is, the best boundary at which to define input. And yet, when we come to the seemingly essential business of saying what it is for two people to be stimulated alike, we tangle with the myth of homologous nerve endings. What will we do when we get to Mars? Just because we and the Martians cannot match up nerve endings, must we despair of relating our languages?

There is an odd irony here. We had been worrying whether scientific sense could be made of mentalistic idioms of propositional attitude, and now we seem unable even to negotiate the A-B-Cs of behavioristic psychology; we are stopped by the notion of a stimulus.

The trouble is really, of course, the intersubjective equating of stimulations. I see no fault in defining the sensory stimulation of a person at a time as the triggering, at that time, of all of a subclass of his sensory receptors. I see no fault, either, in defining a pattern of stimulation of that person simply as a subclass of his sensory receptors; realization of the pattern is then the stimulation that consists in activating all and only the receptors in that subclass. When it comes to the intersubjective, however, perhaps the most we can realistically speak of is resemblance and not identity of stimulation patterns. All stimulation patterns should perhaps be viewed as peculiar to individual subjects, and as bearing intersubjective resemblances, at best, based on approximate homologies of nerve endings. Perhaps the relation of intersubjective stimulus synonymy of observation sentences could be redefined in terms of resemblance rather than identity of stimulus meanings, and finally in terms of near-homology of nerve endings. But this certainly seems a long way around.

All such homology considerations are glaringly theoretical. In practice we usually assure adequately similar stimulation of two subjects by seeing to it that their bodies are reached by similar barrages of outside forces and that the subjects are oriented alike to the stimulus sources and, perhaps, that their eyes are open. On these terms we can even compare a man and a Martian, with never a thought of homologies beyond what little may be required in order to settle on the proper way of orienting the Martian to the stimulus sources.

The Martian might indeed make trouble for us by reacting to forces to which the man is unresponsive and vice versa. The triggering of a receptor is what counts, and this is why the equating of stimulations for two subjects persists in raising homology considerations when we try for an explicit theory. Our rough and ready procedure of simply giving our two subjects similar orientation to similar power sources works well in practice, and for this we can be grateful. It works well because of the anatomical resemblance of people. But for these similarities language itself might not have been propagated.

I leave you, therefore, with a problem of theoretical formulation that carries no evident practical problem with it. It is the problem of saying in general what it means for two subjects to get the same stimulation, or, failing that, what it means for two subjects to get more nearly the same stimulation than two others.

Index